LIVING MY DREAM

DR. HARRY CARTER'S 2006 FIRE ACT ROAD TRIP

USA ▪ Canada ▪ UK ▪ Ireland

Note for Librarians: A cataloguing record for this book is available from Library and Archives Canada at www.collectionscanada.ca/amicus/index-e.html
ISBN 1-4251-0885-7

Offices in Canada, USA, Ireland and UK

Book sales for North America and international:
Trafford Publishing, 6E–2333 Government St.,
Victoria, BC V8T 4P4 CANADA
phone 250 383 6864 (toll-free 1 888 232 4444)
fax 250 383 6804; email to orders@trafford.com
Book sales in Europe:
Trafford Publishing (ᴜᴋ) Limited, 9 Park End Street, 2nd Floor
Oxford, UK OX1 1HH UNITED KINGDOM
phone +44 (0)1865 722 113 (local rate 0845 230 9601)
facsimile +44 (0)1865 722 868; info.uk@trafford.com
Order online at:
trafford.com/06-2643

10 9 8 7 6 5 4 3

Table of Contents

Dedication

This book is dedicated to my best friend, Jack Peltier of Marlborough, Massachusetts. He helped me to frame my thoughts about taking this trip. He put up with me for a month, which is no mean feat. His assistance and companionship made the journey better. His wisdom and guidance kept me going. His thoughtful hints made my writing stronger and better.

A Word of Thanks

At this time it is appropriate to publicly thank a number of organizations and people for their support of the **Road Trip**.

- **Fire and Emergency Manufacturers and Services Association**
- **Fire Apparatus Manufacturers Association**
- **Spartan Motors, Inc.**
- **Amkus Rescue Systems**
- **Class One**
- **Compare USA (MAKO)**
- **Groves, Inc.**
- **Hackney Emergency Vehicles**
- **Hale Products Company**
- **Havis-Shields**
- **Homeland Protection Professional**
- **Paratech**
- **Pierce Manufacturing**
- **Pro Poly of America, Inc.**
- **Total Fire Group**
- **U.S. Tanker**
- **United Plastic Fabricating, Inc.**
- **Waterous Company**
- **Weldon Technologies**
- **Steve Lawrence**
- **Karen Burnham**

Author's Note

"Rare is the American who has not dreamed of dropping whatever he is doing and hitting the road. The dream of unrestrained movement is a distinctly American one" (Nichols, 1989, p. xvii). I have chosen these words from David Nichols edited volume of "Ernie's America: The Best of Ernie Pyle's 1930's Travel Dispatches" to set the tone for this story. I believe it shows that my dream is just one more patch in the crazy quilt that we call America.

This book is about a dream. It is a dream that I have held near to my heart for many years now. That dream involved going on a road trip to visit with members of the American Fire Service. This journey was postponed on many occasions for a myriad of reasons. It was in 2006 that I finally was able to live my dream. How many of you can say that?

Before I get into the meat of my missive, I want to share a few of the motivations which led to the development of my dreams. Unlike many in my generation, I have a great reverence for the past and the lessons which it has to share, if only we would take the time to look for them and listen to the long-stilled voices who uttered them initially.

Many of you will be familiar with my work for Firehouse Magazine. I have been a contributing editor for this fine journal since 1990. I love to read and I love to write. These are two things which go together as naturally as a horse and carriage. Like many of you, I have idols in each sector of my life. There are football idols, fire service idols, and great American idols, like General of the Army Omar Bradley and President Teddy Roosevelt.

One of my idols in the world of writing is a man whose death in 1945 was cause for a national outpouring of grief at his loss.

Ernie Pyle was a native son of Indiana. He was born and raised in Dana, a small farming community in the southwestern part of the state. During his life he traveled and wrote about many different topics. However, it was his travel writings in the 1930's that planted the seed of my road trip back in the late 1980's.

The travel columns to which I make reference were written for the Scripps Howard Newspaper Alliance. His body of work covers the period 1935 to 1942. According to Nash, "...Pyle's roving-reporter pieces answered a need for lighter fare in some American newspapers at a critical time in the nation's history" (Nichols, 1989. p. xxi). His light-hearted, folksy style captured the hearts of readers during the depths of the Great Depression.

He would travel the highways and byways of our nation in search of the real pulse and heartbeat of our nation. He would collect tips and suggestions for interesting people to meet and places to go. He had the Herculean task of creating six 1000-word columns each week. This is far greater than my normal output of about 1,500 words per week for the Firehouse.com website.

This 2006 road trip of mine taught me the value of good notes, discipline, and writing to meet my own self-imposed nightly deadlines. All of the words in this book, with the exception of the first excerpts from my April 2006 Firehouse.com commentary were created on the road. Thanks to the fine folks at Firehouse. com, I had the ability to post to a blog supported by the Cygnus Corporation. I believe that I wrote and posted 47 entries on my blog in just 28 days. This is a workload far beyond normal. However, I did it.

I want to thank my best friend Jack Peltier of Marlborough, Massachusetts for the companionship, help, and guidance he provided to me during our 28-day, 6,194 mile soiree through 18 of these here United States. There were a number of times when I would have gone the wrong way, were it not for Jack's calm demeanor and good direction. Every one needs a best friend like Jack.

It is my hope that Ernie Pyle is somewhere up above smiling down on my efforts to follow in the paths which he blazed seven decades ago. America is still a great land, and the members of the fire service are the best of the best among its citizenry.

I would like to add that all of the proceeds from the sale of this book have been dedicated to the Capital Building Fund of the Colt's Neck Reformed Church in Colts Neck, New Jersey.

Photo: L–R RandyNovak – Iowa Fire Service Training Bureau, Alison Hart – Senator Tom Harkins Staff, Andy McGovern – Training Officer for City of Clinton Fire Department, The Author, Paul Doyle – Training Officer City of Goose Lake Fire Department, Kevin Cain – Chief Officer City of Goose Lake Fire Department

Harry Carter's 2006 Fire Act Road Trip

2006 has been a pretty good year for the Carter Family. The third weekend in February was a real treat for my family and me. My wife and two daughters flew out with me to Anaheim, California to attend the commencement ceremony for Capella University. Folks, I swore to myself that when I finally finished my doctoral program, I was going to walk at the school's graduation ceremony.

After three fairly intense years of study and preparation, that joyous day finally arrived. When the school offered me the opportunity to travel to Anaheim or Minneapolis for the festivities, I left the choice to my family. I asked them which ceremony they would rather attend: Anaheim in February or Minneapolis in August. It really was no surprise to me when they chose Anaheim.

The answer should have been obvious. Do you remember the Super Bowl commercials where the MVP of the game was asked where he was going to celebrate his victory? I know I do. Invariably the answer would be something with the word Disney attached to it.

Guess what my friends? When I graduated from Capella I went to Disneyland. Truth be told; I think I like Disney World a bit better. But that minor bias did not stop me from enjoying the Pirates of the Caribbean, visiting the "It's a small world" pavilion, listening to the Firehouse Five Dixieland music ensemble, or riding a horse on the Carousel.

On the flight (very long because of headwinds) out to the John Wayne Airport in Anaheim we were treated to three consecutive movies (yes it was a long trip). I loved Elf. I always get a kick out of Will Ferrell. The last feature just made no impression on me so I did not watch it. However, it was the first and newest movie, Elizabethtown, which caused the bright light of a fresh thought to flash on within the belfry of my mind, thereby driving the bats out into the cabin of Continental Flight 387. What a great moment.

Once the flight attendant and I were able to gather the belfry bats up into a convenient plastic bag, and tuck them in a small compartment, I whipped out my handy dandy laptop computer and let the good times roll. The movie was really neat. Even though I am not normally a fan of first run movies, this movie caught my attention.

Elizabethtown started off somewhat slowly. A great personal failure on the hero's part is followed by the death of his father. My first thought was that the story was going to be a real downer. However, as the plot began to unfold, my opinion quickly changed. It turned out to be an interesting tale playing off personal failure against the twin themes of hope and love. Being the incurable romantic that I am, I rooted for the hero (Orlando Bloom) to hook up with the heroine (Kirsten Dunst).

During the journey from failure to success and love, one thought kept running through my mind. It seemed as though the movie's creators were saying that failure is the starting point for success in the future. As you may recall, this has been a recurring theme in my writing over the past decade. The movie reinforced my view of that part of the world.

Now comes the part that really made me think. The concluding segments of the movie revolved around a road trip which takes the hero across the highways and byways of our nation. The love interest (Dunst) structures the trip in such a way that the hero is allowed to explore the parameters of his troubled life, while at the same time seeing some of the neat sites of the mid-south.

The trip takes him west from Kentucky. I absolutely loved the scenes where Bloom rolled down the highways and byways of Middle America jamming to the sounds of some really great blues tunes. The scenes in Memphis evoked a real sense of nostalgia in my airborne psyche. They took me back to the days when the Fire Department Instructors Conference was still held in that great city by the Mississippi. It was really neat.

It came to me as our aircraft winged its way westward that the person who created this movie was on to something. What better way to come in contact with your soul than rolling across our great nation at the wheel of a modern, metal chariot. Somewhere well above the very same roads of Middle America which were being shown in the movie, a really neat thought came to me.

Like the hero of the movie I too need to do a road trip. I need to travel the highways and byways of our great nation. I need to meet you. What a great way to see and assess what you are thinking than meeting up with you folks out there across America on your own turf. What better way to see what you folks are really doing out there in America. I believe that I need to get out there and meet with you.

I have written much about the journey of our fire service through the past 30 years. However, I have long felt that something was missing: the personal touch. The American Fire

Service that I know so well is in reality a group of probably 4,000 to 5,000 people who are regular attendees at the major fire conferences held around the country. I see them at the FDIC, IAFC, and Firehouse Expo conferences. They regularly work the circuit, making their pilgrimage to the various venues along with me.

During this road trip it would be my intention to meet with some of the people who really get the job done in their hometowns. These would be the people like those with whom I regularly work in Western Monmouth County, New Jersey. They go to work. They protect their communities and lead fairly regular lives. What are their hopes and dreams? Where do they think the fire service should be headed?

There is also another reason for my journey. It came up one morning at breakfast in Indianapolis during the recent Fire Department Instructor's Conference. My best buddy Jack Peltier suggested that I should go out and meet a number of those departments who have benefited from the grants provided by the Assistance to Firefighters program created by the FIRE Act legislation. These success stories, he felt, are critical to the future of the program.

Like you, I have heard a number of success stories, but my heart tells me that there are more. I need to write these things down, take some pictures, and share all of these thoughts with the fire service. What better way to justify more funding than to create a journal that tells our Senators and our Congress people about the true value of this program.

I already have people from the following states who have invited me to come and see their success. So far I am planning to head on out to:

- New Jersey
- Pennsylvania
- Ohio
- Indiana
- Illinois
- Tennessee
- West Virginia
- Virginia
- Maryland
- Delaware

I have lined up some support in this effort. So far the following people and organizations have offered their assistance:

- Bobby Halton of Fire Engineering magazine
- Chris Hebert of Firehouse.com
- Dan Jones of National Fire Rescue News
- Janet Wilmoth of Fire Chief magazine

I have also received an offer of help from Barry Balliet, President of the Provident Insurance Company. I am hoping that some of the other folks who have benefited from the success of the program will step forward and support my effort to tell the true story of the FIRE Act.

It is my plan to create a pamphlet which tells the story of the success of the Fire Act program. After I explained my idea to him at the FDIC in Indianapolis, Dennis Compton asked me to deliver a paper on my trip to the Washington, DC research conference in January where the latest round of papers based upon the fire prevention grants provided under the provisions of the Fire Act will be presented.

Along the way I will be creating a daily web log for Firehouse. com, as well as weekly reports for all of the media outlets. There will also be a series of articles on my journey. All of these will be available for you to use in contacting your Senators and Members of Congress. Heck, I would like to meet your local members of Congress and the Senate. Do not forget the people who write for your local newspapers and the people on your local television stations.

My goal is really quite simple. The current administration is trying to take away our FIRE Act money. People are scrambling to come up with ways to show the value of the program. I want to make a difference. What better way could there be that to create a short, easy-to-read pamphlet featuring the people who have seen their organizations prosper because of the funds granted to them by the Assistance to Firefighters grant program?

Of course this trip might never come off. Life has a way of tossing each of us curve balls as we move through life. Who knows? However, it is up to you to help me make the decision. If you have a place where a couple of people might be able to gather, where you and I could meet and where I might be able to lecture and pass the hat for gas money, please send me a note. I also want to write about you.

One of my great literary heroes, the late World War II war correspondent Ernie Pyle, became famous before the war by traveling the roads of America during the 1930's writing about the people he met along the way. I have read and reread the book which covers his travels and his life as a newspaper man. It just seems really interesting to hit the road and write about the people you meet.

My goal is to travel from New Jersey to points north, west, and south (East would be very wet). I have been putting this trip off for a long time now. Perhaps it is time to mount up on my trusty GMC chariot and roll westward, leaving a cloud of cigar smoke and circus music in my wake. If you think this is a good idea, please drop me an email and share your thoughts. Perhaps I shall acquire a CD which numbers Willie Nelson's famous "On the Road Again" among its selections.

Anyway, Mrs. Carter just said that I can go. So I want to get rolling. I am thinking about doing this in late June and early July. Let me know what you think. Contact your suppliers and distributors and ask them to contact the big companies. You and I can make this happen.

Please bear with me my friends. These are but the ramblings of a brand-new, 58-year-old University graduate. I want you to know one important fact of life. It is just like inscription on the statue of Emil Faber in the 1978 movie classic Animal House: "Knowledge is Good." Take care my friends and have a great week.

Hershey, Pennsylvania July 6, 2006

A Great Way to Kick Off the Trip with a Train Wreck

Hershey is a lovely community located in Central Pennsylvania, not far from the state Capitol in Harrisburg. Farms abound in this area. As a matter of fact, the route into town ran through a continuing sea of corn growing on both sides of the road. I thought that maybe all of this corn was growing in response to the burgeoning ethanol industry in our nation. Such is not the case. The bulk of the corn is used to feed the cows on the dairy farms that surround Hershey.

One needs to look no further than the massive Hershey Company manufacturing complexes in three different areas of Upper Derry Township to see why there might be a major-league requirement for lots of milk. Maybe you are like me and thought that the actual name of the town was Hershey. Such is not the case.

There was a move to change the name from Upper Derry Township to Hershey.

Leading the battle against this change was the local historical association. After the won the referendum to maintain the traditional Upper Derby name, they promptly change their name to the Hershey Historical Association. My sources suggest that they did this to better attract grant funding for their programs.

The Hershey Volunteer Fire Department is a product of the fertile mind of Milton Hershey, the founder and creator of the chocolate manufacturing dynasty which bears his name. Local lore has it that Hershey suffered a fire loss at one of his facilities. He noted the lack of a local fire department and worked to found it in 1905. Here are some of the historical facts which surround the formation of this all-volunteer entity which I extracted from their website:

August 31st, 1905 – The first organizational meeting was held in a car barn on East Chocolate Avenue across from the Chocolate factory, 33 men attended.

February 4th, 1906 – The Fire Company is permanently organized and moved into a building on East Chocolate Avenue next to the Chocolate Factory. The site was later the location of the Post Office and is now vacant.

February 17th, 1907 – Official charter granted – This carries the names of 73 men including Milton S. Hershey. He proved to be a great benefactor to the company.

June 23rd, 1928 – A new firehouse was dedicated. It was built on land donated by Mr. Hershey. This remains the center section of the current firehouse.

We met our host Lt. Rodney Sonderman at the fire station located in the downtown area at 21 West Caracas Street, near

Cocoa Street. Oddly enough they are located on block away from Chocolate Ave. However, before he arrived, we had the privilege to chat with a number of department members who were more than happy to show us the good things which the FIRE Act had allowed them to do. The first thing I noted was that they had installed a complete automatic fire sprinkler protection system in their decades-old fire station. In light of the fact that more than 100 firehouses are damaged to some extent each year by fire, this impressed me as a very good move on the part of the Hershey Volunteer Fire Department.

These kind firefighters, who had all been up for many hours during the night, then went on to show me the on-board computers installed on all of the equipment. It was at this point that Lt. Sonderman arrived and took us to observe the on-going rail incident.

It seems that one of the major items funded by the FIRE Act was a fire safety house to teach school children how to be safe in the event of fire. Since the schools were not in session, the Hershey Volunteer Fire Department rolled this unit to the scene to serve as a command post for the incident. When we arrived, the computers and printers were busy spitting out hourly up date reports and photos for the command staff.

Jack and I were then briefed by the Incident Commander, Assistant Chief Jason Hottenstein. Both he and Lt. Sonderman made a point of describing the way in which the on-board computers and global-positioning systems, funded by the FIRE Act, were of tremendous value during the initial stages of the operation.

It seems that as Lt. Sonderman, serving as the Department's Duty Officer arrived at the incident, he encountered a sight not often seen. He saw a great many railroad tank cars scattered about the scene like so many toys tossed about by a giant. He quickly entered the location data into the computer in his vehicle.

He then stepped out of his vehicle and counted the number of derailed cars.

He also noted that a great many hazardous materials placards were present and was able to determine that the greatest hazard came from a derailed and overturned chlorine tanker. Once he made this determination, he was able to quickly determine the area within the 1,000-foot evacuation radius that had to be addressed. He then passed that information to the Incident Commander who determined that an evacuation was in order. The initial evacuation was then begun.

As the incident grew in size and complexity, the computer and GPS equipment proved invaluable. It allowed them to expand the size of the evacuation area by the touch of a few key strokes. The equipment was so precise that the command staff was able to assign fire personnel to evacuate the nearby homes and businesses by street address.

I mentioned all of this to Brent Sailhamer, Community and Economic Development Coordinator for United States Senator Rick Santorum during a meeting at the Senator's office in Harrisburg later in the afternoon. What better example of the good works provided by the FIRE Act funding than to see the equipment purchased by the act working to protect lives and assist in keeping the flow of interstate rail commerce flowing through Central Pennsylvania. Mr. Sailhamer was a most gracious host, and assured me that my message would be carried forward to the Senator.

After our meeting we returned to Hershey for another look at the scene. We noted further updates to the maps and photos, and watched the railroad recovery crews raise a tank car and place it on a new set of trucks. All the while things continued to operate smoothly at the multi-agency, unified command post. I left the scene confident that these talented men and women would continue to work valiantly on behalf of the citizens of Hershey.

As I write these words for you, decisions are being made as to how to off-load product. The staff of the Hershey Volunteer Fire Department will be spending another rough night at the scene. I firmly believe that things went a heck of a lot better at this incident because of the equipment provided by the largess of the FIRE Act. Who knows what tomorrow will bring in Johnstown, Pennsylvania.

Johnstown, Pennsylvania July 7, 2006

A County Team is Born

L et me start today's entry with a simple statement. Johnstown welcomed me with open arms on a quiet afternoon. After winding our way over a series of state highways, and climbing a couple of thousand feet up into the air, Jack and I arrived to find a nice, quite, sunny afternoon in Johnstown after winding down the other side of the mountains that circle the city.

Johnstown is a famous place in American History. Unfortunately it is famous for the three floods which ravaged the city at various times during its history. The Great Flood in 1889 is the one that gained the greatest attention. However, other major floods in 1936 and 1977 caused a great deal of damage.

Over the years, coal, steel, and iron played an important part in the development of the city. At one point, Johnstown was the leading producer of steel in America. One its greatest manufacturing products produced during the 1800's was barbed wire. It produced most of our nation's barbed wire during the latter part of the 19th Century.

The city saw its peaks years as a steel producer during the post-World War II period. However, increased domestic and foreign competition, coupled with Johnstown's relative distance from its primary iron ore source in the western Great Lakes, led to a steady decline in profitability. Today Johnstown can best be described as a city on the rebound.

Brian Feist, Executive Director of the Cambria County Department of Emergency Services was a most accommodating host. Shortly after my arrival he introduced me to the members of all four local television stations. I spent a number moments answering the questions posed to me. As a matter of fact I ended up as the lead story on a number of the local television stations.

I met a number of local government leaders from the City of Johnstown and Cambria County. I also met a representative from Senator Arlen Spector's office, as well as the district representative from Congressman Bill Shuster's Hollidaysburg office. I explained that the purpose of my road trip was to meet people who had benefited from the FIRE Act. I asked them all to work together to tell this story to their Members of Congress.

After answering a number of really interesting questions, Brian took me to the new county emergency service complex for the most important part of my visit. I spent a number of hours interviewing local fire department members whose agencies had received FIRE Act assistance funding. I met with:

- Fire Chief Tony Kovacic of Johnstown
- Chief Joe Huber of the Hastings Volunteer Fire Department
- Chief Paul Kundrod of the St. Michael Volunteer Fire Department
- Assistant Chief Brian Feist of the Conemaugh Volunteer Fire Department

- Firefighters Mike Starchville and Ted Beck of the
  Cassandra Volunteer Fire Department

Each person spoke of the impact that the grants had made upon their departments. Over the course of our interviews a number of salient points were touched. The list of items acquired involved a wide range of protective equipment, apparatus, and other important things.

One special piece of equipment that stood out was the mobile communications unit created for the Johnstown Fire Department with FIRE Act funding. It serves as the focal point for all communications and interoperability issues in the region. It can set up a satellite downlink service for data receipt and transmission. It can allow communications between units from different organizations and band spectrums. It also can create a satellite voice communications unit and serve as a wireless Internet hot spot for other units on scene.

It is equipment such as this which multiplies the impact of the FIRE Act funding over their entire region. This valuable unit has even been selected to provide communication's support for the Major League Baseball All-Star game at PNC Park in Pittsburgh. It is responding to provide an expanded communications capability for this important national event.

The one point which stood out among many identified during the course of the interviews involved two critical elements of operational importance. Each of the people spoke to the fact that the morale of their organizations was improved by the infusion of federal money. This will surely help in the recruiting and retention of department members.

One person stated that their people were pleased to all look the same for the first time in their history. They got rid of turnout gear and SCBA equipment that was more than twenty years old. The entire group felt that the improved safety equipment allowed each member to feel that they could operate more effectively, efficiently, and safely.

Another prevalent opinion revolved around the fact that the federal money allowed the individual departments to take a little time away from their intensive fund-raising efforts. Each department was able to raise the overall training level of their departments.

Johnstown was also able to educate all of its fire personnel to serve as fire inspectors. In addition they used funding from one of the grants to create a community smoke detector program. Not long after the first detectors were issued, a fire occurred, which in the days before the detector program would have been a room and contents fire with a loss of around $2,500 according to Chief Kovacic of Johnstown. The actual number was around $250. The FIRE Act money was directly returned to the community in the form of better service.

I would like to make one more observation on my visit to Cambria County. There is a spirit of cooperation that other areas could do well emulate. I would suggest that they look to Brian Feist and his associates as a model for administrative mutual aid. One person helps the other to get their grant application in shape. Of course like any other place there are those people who wish to have no help from Big Brother. People were described to me that I will swear I already knew.

Anyway, I am pleased to report a most successful soiree into the Allegheny Mountain region of the Commonwealth of Pennsylvania. I was privileged to meet some really dedicated members of our fire service.

Incidentally, Rodney Sonderman called me just before the 1300 hr. press conference to let me know that the Hershey incident has been terminated around 1200 hr. He was pleased to report that there were no injuries to anyone during the course of the operation. Congratulations on a great job.

Poland/Boardman, Ohio July 8, 2006

A Quiet Saturday and a Backyard Picnic

O urs is a trip of discovery. It was our original intention to discover things about the FIRE Act and its impact upon the American Fire Service. However, whenever you depart on a trip it is hard to tell exactly what you might discover during any given day.

This proved true once again as Jack Peltier and I were making our way down U.S. Route #22 in western Pennsylvania. I forget exactly which town we were passing through when a business sign caught our attention. The sign said Climax the discreet men's club. Of course this would attract our attention. We are guys. However the next sign almost stopped us dead in our tracks.

The next sign said Climax, the "drive-in" gentleman's club. I am neither a novice nor a prude, but it just seemed like we should stop and see how they managed to pull off that act of free enterprise within the Commonwealth of Pennsylvania. Rest assured my friends that we chose not to stop.

I will always wonder, though. Just how do you deliver that particular product in the manner described? Ah, but that is for another time and another trip. We had to push on to meet with the officers and members of the Western Reserve Joint Fire District in Poland, Ohio.

Founded in 1923, the department has a force of 85 members operating out of three stations. The have a diverse fleet of ten units which handle fire, rescue, and EMS responses.

Poland is not a new community by a long shot. It is a 21-square mile area located in the suburbs just to the south of Youngstown. According to our host, Chief David "Chip" Comstock, the original inhabitants of the community were veterans of the Revolutionary War who moved west to accept land grants which given to them as a reward for their service in our War of Independence. They moved into an area whose land had been surveyed and marked out by men who were trained by George Washington himself.

Local lore also mentions that President McKinley took the oath of enlistment to join the union army in a building not too many doors down from the current fire headquarters. He then left Ohio to fight for the Union.

You will be pleased to learn that there was no major disaster awaiting our arrival. Our meeting with the fine folks in Poland, Ohio was conducted under the most cordial of circumstances. I was most fortunate indeed to arrive in town on the day of the fire department's annual golf outing and picnic.

I did not make the golf tournament, but I sure as heck made an appearance at the picnic. Tony Tucci was kind enough to host the festivities at his home in the northeast side of the community. The steaks were done to a turn and there were enough different desserts to meet the taste of any sugar addict in the world.

Guess what my friends? A fireman's picnic in Ohio is strikingly similar to other such affairs I have attended in a number of different states. I broke bread with some really neat, caring, sharing individuals. Jack and I were greeted like a couple of long-lost friends.

As the afternoon turned into evening, the storytelling was ratcheted up several notches. We traded war stories, family stories, and eventually segued into a retelling of the Great Bakersfield 99-Mile Mutual Aid Trip. This is a critical story because it goes to the heart of the impact of the FIRE Act upon the Western Reserve Joint Fire District and a number of their surrounding mutual aid partners.

The department was part of a consortium that went together during the 2004 grant cycle to request a total of 155 self-contained breathing units with masks that have voice amplification. The grant also allowed the departments involved to acquire the technology to monitor the individuals wearing the SCBA during emergency operations.

Thanks to a series of consoles and laptop computers, the command vehicle can monitor the members who are on air. The system can read the air pressure levels in the tanks, and can be used to initiate a building evacuation by sending a tone to each unit. It can also receive a distress signal in the event that a member goes down. The end result of this is a much higher level of safety for the members of the regional mutual aid compact.

They did not want to waste the opportunity to assist fire departments who were less fortunate than they are, so they put together a program to donate the units which were replaced to other fire departments. This led to a 99-mile trip to Bakersfield, Ohio. When the members from Western Reserve arrived in the small rural community to the south of Poland, they found a fire department with only nine SCBA units, six of which were inoperable.

When they left, that department had ten SCBA units which were compliant with the appropriate codes and standards. While there they responded on their Squad truck along with the

Bakersfield brush unit to a fire involving hay in a barn next to a chicken coop. The story is that thanks to their efforts, more than 20,000 chickens were saved. That's their story and they are sticking to it.

The Western Reserve Joint Fire District received FIRE Act assistance in 2002, 2004, and 2005. Chief Comstock mentioned that the first grant in 2002 was critical in changing the direction of the department. The money was used for upgrading the training level of departmental members. Most members of the department are now trained to the more stringent Ohio Firefighter II level. He also said that increase in organizational pride was a great thing to see.

Once again I noted a couple of critical elements of organizational success which were engendered by the FIRE Act. There was a palpable increase in departmental pride. My research indicates that pride is a critical element in the recruiting and retention efforts of every fire department. These folks are now better trained and equipped to protect their community and proud of the way in which they now can do their jobs. The discussions indicated that there was also an improvement in the inter-community relationships among the cooperating agencies.

I also got to see an excellent example of the FIRE Act helping a major city that is undergoing tough financial times. Like many areas, the Youngtown, Ohio region, has fallen on hard economic times as the major industries have shuttered their doors and moved away from the city.

In a like manner so too have the fortunes of their fire department fallen. They have closed stations, lost staff, and have been generally forced into a period of retrenchment. Thanks to the FIRE Act program they have been able to acquire necessary equipment and apparatus that they otherwise would never have been able to receive.

I also got to meet a real neat guy from the Cleveland Fire

Department. His name is Ken Shupe and he does a great deal of teaching around the U.S. He has worked at the Fire Department Instructor's Conference (FDIC) for a number of years now and will shortly have an article published in Fire Engineering magazine. We shared some really great, rust-belt, big city war stories. It is nice to know another man out there who has a passion for teaching, training, and sharing.

Once again I discovered another organization that the FIRE Act had helped. It has sure made a great difference to a number of communities in Eastern Ohio. To Chip Comstock, Sonny Chinowth, Tony Tucci and all of the members of the Western Reserve Joint Fire District, thank you for your hospitality and good luck with this year's FIRE Act competition.

New Knoxville, Ohio July 9, 2006

A Neat Small Town and a Number of Progressive Fire Departments

This day's journey saw Jack and me heading west from Poland, Ohio. The trip across Ohio convinced us that there is still a great deal of open land in America. We zoomed past mile after mile of simply beautiful farmland. The traffic was not bad at all and we made very good time traveling over Interstate 76 to U.S. 30 and on down Interstate 76. Many of the miles we traveled were probably traversed during the 1930's by my literary hero, the late Ernie Pyle.

I can recall sections of his travelogues where he spoke of traveling along the Lincoln Highway. I too spent a bit of time this day traveling along that same old Lincoln Highway route. Let me share a few facts about this famous man.

"Pyle studied journalism at Indiana University and left school to become a reporter for a small-town newspaper. In 1935, after various editorial jobs, he acquired a roving assignment for the Scripps-Howard newspaper chain. His daily experiences furnished him with material for a column that eventually appeared in 200 newspapers" (American Writer.org).

His writing entertained a generation of Americans who were struggling through the Great Depression. It also serves as a descriptive legacy of an era that long ago disappeared from the face of out nations.

After about five comfortable hours of driving, Jack and I worked our way over a series of smaller state and county roads to New Knoxville, Ohio. Since we were a bit early for our meeting with Chief Scott Schroer and his training officer Jerry Merges, we decided to stop in for a bit of lunch at a local eating establishment.

Stepping through the doors of the Main Street Station restaurant took us on a journey back in time. This had to be what small town eateries were like during the 1940's. The walls were lined with class pictures from New Knoxville High School dating back to the 1940's. There were also photos of championship sports teams and local luminaries.

My eye was attracted to a plaque commemorating those scores of local men and women who served in World War II. Special mention was made of those who were killed during their service. Below was a statement from the local manufacturing firm that sponsored the plaque. It read, "The Hoge Brush Company helped win World War II." My friends that firm is still going strong in New Knoxville.

Jack happened to be wearing his Massachusetts Firefighting Academy polo shirt. When the waitress came up to give us our menus, she looked at Jack and asked if he was from Massachusetts. His affirmative answer led her to tell Jack and me that she was from Sudbury, a town less than ten miles from Jack. Talk about a small world.

Chief Schroer and Jerry Merges had managed to assemble an

interesting array of local fire service leaders from their mutual aid area. Jack and I met with Chief Schroer and Jerry Merges from the New Knoxville department, as well as Chief Jerome Barhorst from the Fort Loramie Community Fire Department and Chief Mark Seitz of the Chickasaw Community Mutual Fire Company.

Over the course of our interviews the importance of the FIRE Act program came alive as each of these dedicated men spoke of the changes that the funding had made. Once again I observed a sense of real camaraderie among the discussion participants.

They have grown closer together as a result of their efforts to help each other learn about the grant process. They took turns reviewing each others applications and offered suggestions as appropriate. These are fire departments which respond together on a regular, mutual aid basis.

Chief Seitz has spent a great deal of time attending FEMA training sessions on the grant process. He is looked upon as a bit of a FIRE Act guru.

I was fortunate to have Chief Barhorst sitting next to me. He was my first interview candidate and really jumped in with both feet. His praise for the program was high indeed. Mark Seitz was next up and opined that the funding had allowed his department to take a bit of time away from fund-raising. Chief Schroer and Jerry Merges outlined the response improvements they have been able to enjoy thanks to the grant funding.

These departments now all have similar turnout gear, identical self-contained breathing apparatus, new radios on the same frequency, as well as identical rescue tools. Each chief noted that they are now able to cover their own territories a lot better and work far more closely on a mutual aid basis.

It should be noted that while these great similarities exist, they were not all funded by FIRE Act money. The new equipment acquired with the assistance money was specifically matched up to the existing units for greater ease of interoperability.

My friends, these are not large communities. These are smaller rural areas which are a long way away from any large city. However, they have a job to do and require the same tools as their colleagues in the big cities to get that job done. It is just like Chief Seitz said. "We need the same tools to fight a fire in a two-story building that New York City needs. The FIRE Act has allowed us to get them."

Recently a major fire in Chief Barhorst's district required the combined efforts of at least 18 different fire departments. More than 1,000,000 gallons of water was pumped over the course of the operation. The chief told us that probably 17 of the 18 departments had received some form of FIRE Act assistance over the past five years. A lot of the equipment used in that effort might not have been available without the FIRE Act.

Sadly, a tragedy in the not-too-distant past has brought all of the fire people in this area together. About two years ago, John Garman and Ken Jutte of the New Bremen Fire Department died in the line of duty during a silo fire in that community. Each of the men around the table with me was part of that sad operation. They were all deeply affected.

Chief Schroer said it best for the group when he told me that he was going to do his level best to provide his people with the best training and equipment possible. Each of the chiefs mirrored his sentiments. Thanks to the FIRE Act, these chiefs have been able to make good on many of their promises.

Xenia, Ohio July 10, 2006

The Home of Major League Regional Interoperability

Today was another joy for Jack and me. However it did not turn out as we thought it would. It was just one of those things that I felt might happen over the course of a four-week tour. We were headed for one town and ended up in another.

Thankfully Chief Mark Wolf of Greenville, Ohio is a flexible individual indeed. I was headed for his community for a morning appointment. Prior to pulling out of the parking lot at the Hampton Inn in Sidney I paused to call Chief Tim Spradlin of the Xenia Township Fire Department. I wanted to firm up our Tuesday appointment. What to my wondering ears did occur but a message of wonderment on Tim's part.

Apparently there was a mix-up somewhere along the line and he told me that he had set up a big event with the local media. There were also a half dozen local fire chiefs due in to meet me. How could this have happened? I told him not to worry. I would figure something out.

I immediately called Chief Wolf and asked for an accommodation. I outlined the error and he proved to be most gracious indeed. He was kind enough to postpone our meeting until tomorrow. What a kind and understanding person. I look forward to meeting with him.

With that little bump in the road paved over, Jack and I took off for Xenia. As we cruised on down Interstate 75 headed south, I put in a call to Chief Spradlin. He was pleased that I was en route and then dictated a series of shortcuts to Jack over the phone.

Not too long after that we motored into the Old Town section of Xenia Township. Yet again Jack and I marveled at the pristine beauty of this small slice of our great nation. After a tour of the township station in Old Town, we took off for Beautiful Downtown Xenia.

Founded in 1803 Xenia has enjoyed a long and prosperous life in the western part of Ohio. It contains a mixture of residential areas, light industry, and several educational facilities. It is interesting to note that the name Xenia comes from the Greek word for hospitality.

Sure enough, the first welcome sign we saw told us that we were entering Xenia, Ohio: The City of Hospitality. If the greeting I received from the local troops means anything, they made me a true believer that there was much more to that sign than mere words.

My co-hosts for the visit were Chief Jeff Leaming of the Xenia City Fire Department and Chief W.T. "Tim" Spradlin of the Xenia Township Fire Department. The city forms a traditional type of hole within the donut relationship with the township. This geographical fact has led to an excellent hand-in-glove relationship between the two communities.

Once again I was the subject of a television news interview.

Before my meeting with the fire chiefs began I had the privilege of meeting TV-7 Newswoman Gabrielle Enright. She was kind enough to interview me for a spot on the evening news in Dayton. I spoke of the importance of the FIRE Act and, since Tim Spradlin had briefed me on the impact in his area, of the good things that it had done for the fire departments in Green County.

Gabbie, as the firefighters call her, then interviewed Fairborn Chief Mike Riley and me. Mike is the President of the Green County Fire Chief's Association. We discussed the impact of the joint FIRE Act grant that funded an 800-megahertz radio system for most of the county. When combined with the existing capabilities of the City of Xenia, it allowed for the creation of a complete, seamless system of communications for the county.

After the TV interview I spoke with the assembled chiefs from the county who were kind enough to take time from their regular, busy schedules. I explained the history of the act and my involvement in the meetings to help set up the act in 2000. I then held a round-robin discussion with all assembled about the impacts of the grant in their individual communities. Taking part in this session were:

- Chief Jeff Leaming and Captains Ken Riggsby and Douglas Cope, and of the City of Xenia Fire Department
- Chief Tim Spradlin and Captain Steve Helling of the Xenia Township Fire Department
- Chief Scott Baldwin of the Cedarville Township Volunteer Fire Department
- Chief Randall Pavlak of the Sugarcreek Township Fire Department
- Chief Tony Tidd of the New Jasper Township Fire and EMS

- Chief Mike Riley of the Fairborn Fire Department
- Chief Mark Thomas and Firefighter Nathan Hiester of the Beavercreek Township Fire Department
- Roseann Anders from the Green County Emergency Management Agency (Known to one and all as the Grant's Queen)
- Major Eric Prindle of the Green County Sheriff's Office

These kind souls conducted a fast-paced discussion of the impact that FIRE Act funding had upon their departments. Each spoke of the individual items acquired by their agency and then came together as a group to praise the efforts of Chief Pavalak of Sugarcreek.

It seems that his department was the one which served as the central focus for the largest Fire Act grant ever received in Ohio. This communications-based effort allowed everyone in the county to receive sufficient equipment to allow every rig to have a new 800 MHZ mobile radio and portable radios for every riding position. While this in itself is a fabulous achievement, it was only the beginning.

Committees were created to allow for better operational planning to take place throughout the county. There are now common RIT team policies, accountability systems and radio dispatch procedures which provide a great deal of cross-border support for every incident in the region.

These departments are now able to talk to each other at all times and places. They also have a mobile command unit which allows anyone arriving at the scene of an incident who is not on the system to have their radios cloned into the operational frequencies. It should be noted that Green County has been innovative in the use of FIRE Act funding as the basis for other grants which Roseann Anders has secured through the county EMA program.

Chief Pavak was most passionate in his argument for a greater

FIRE Act emphasis on regional efforts like his. Scott Baldwin's fire department acquired a mobile burn building with their FIRE Act money. They now serve as an active training resource not only for their own department but for Green County, as well as a number of surrounding counties. The Beavercreek grant served as the catalyst for regional cooperation.

This sort of a grant has had a fabulous multiplier effect for the region. More than that, other states and members of the federal government have come to Green County to see how their programs work. Stronger bridges have been built to the Fire Department at Wright-Patterson Air Force Base. The federal people are building radio bridges to the county which allow for a smoother mutual aid interaction. What was always good is now better.

One word kept coming up as a common thread throughout the discussions. That word was camaraderie. Each person with whom I spoke made reference to the area-wide teamwork that is now in play. I see this as a trend in each of the places I have visited. Perhaps this is an unforeseen positive effect of the FIRE Act.

Tony Tidd spoke a great deal about the positive impact of the grant funding on local department members. Scott Baldwin and all of the others echoed his comments. Since their members were safer in their new gear and better able to interact through their communications equipment, each felt that their members were safer and thereby better able to support their communities.

After the group session was completed, I met with each of the chiefs individually and conducted a series of tape-recorded interviews. I will use these to draft my report on the overall road trip.

A number of us remained to watch Gabrielle on the TV 7 Five O'Clock News. She did a beautiful job, if I must say so myself.

Jack and I returned to the Interstate by way of the Cedarville fire station. We inspected the mobile burn building and took a look at Scott Baldwin's apparatus fleet. Scott has built a really neat fleet by buying top-quality used fire apparatus.

After a quick goodbye, we left for our overnight destination in Troy. Off to Greenville in the morning.

Greenville, Ohio July 11, 2006

With FIRE Act Money, New SCBA Equals Confidence to Get the Job Done

T oday was the first day when rain crossed our path. From the looks of the grass and crops we saw over the past two days, this rain was a true blessing from above. Our journey this morning took us through a number of small communities where agriculture is the main local industry.

All of a sudden we emerged from the farmlands and found ourselves in the midst of Greenville, Ohio, a thriving small regional center. As we moved down the main street I saw something I haven't seen in years. There was angled parking all along the main drag. More than that we did not see a vacant shop or store as we moved through the city.

According to local historians Greenville first established its pivotal location in America's heartland in 1793, when General Anthony Wayne chose the site as his base to establish control over the Great Northwest Territory. It was here that Wayne's army constructed its headquarters, Fort Greene Ville, naming it after Wayne's war co-patriot General Nathanael Greene.

Covering 50 acres, Fort Greene Ville was the largest log blockhouse fort constructed in the territory northwest of the Ohio River. Within the walls of this fort, Wayne negotiated the famous Treaty of Greene Ville, whereby the proud Native Americans, formerly allied with British, acknowledged themselves to be under the protection of the United States, and no other Power whatever.

According to Mayor Greg Fraley, in the 21st century, Greenville looks to become a leader among rural communities in quality of life, economic development, education, safety, and government services. Greenville is the home of the Kitchen Aid Stand Mixer, international suppliers BASF and Greenville Technology Incorporated, Honeywell/Fram and Beauty Systems Group, Inc. The City of Greenville was ranked one of America's Top 100 Small Towns for Corporate Locations by *Site Selection* magazine.

The Greenville which we found upon our arrival was every bit the active regional center. We met Fire Chief Mark Wolf at fire headquarters which is located right off of one of the largest, best-maintained, and most polite traffic circles it has ever been my pleasure to drive around.

The primary items acquired with the FIRE Act funding were a complete new set of self-contain breathing apparatus (SCBA) and a full set of rescue tools. Like many departments, different brands of SCBA had been acquired over the years at a variety of times. Chief Wolf stated that it was his intention to correct that problem when he was appointed as the Chief. However he noted that it would probably have taken 15 years to replace the existing SCBA under their existing capital improvement plan. Imagine the problems which might crop up with the SCBA as time went by.

Chief Wolf also mentioned that the department's rescue capability was virtually non-existent prior to the FIRE Act grant award. "We went from no tools, to new tools thanks to the FIRE Act," he noted. The department went from practically no equipment to a full set of the appropriate rescue tools. He mentioned that they would often have to wait quite awhile for such equipment to come from a neighboring community.

One of the great improvements which came about as a result of these grant-funded items was in the area of confidence among the personnel. The chief mentioned that at any given time a person might have been wearing any one of the four different kinds of SCBA. Imagine the problems that a malfunction could have caused under those circumstances. "My firefighters have a great deal more confidence in their ability to get the job done now," Chief Wolf added.

Along with the improved level of confidence comes an improved level of safety for the firefighters. When a person feels better about their ability to get the job done, the citizens of the community will experience a higher level of service from their fire department.

After our interview, Chief Wolf introduced Jack and I to Jeff Frech, one of his full-time firefighters. He mentioned that Jeff was the Chief of the neighboring volunteer fire department in New Madison. In our discussions Jeff Frech mentioned that as a result of the FIRE Act, his community had replaced all of their SCBA and also acquired a new compressor.

It is important to note that the two departments both acquired the same brand of SCBA from their FIRE Act grants. They are now completely interoperable in terms of SCBA and refill capability. Both Chief Wolf and Jeff Frech noted that every fire department in Darke County has received at least one grant.

Prior to our arrival Chief Wolfe had gotten information from a number of other fire departments. My thanks go out to Chief

Colin Altman of the Miami Township Fire-Rescue and Chief Doug Cothran of the Rossburg Volunteer Fire Department for sending along information on their FIRE Act grant awards.

Each department wrote of the importance of the grants in changing the way things operate in their community. Miami Township received funding for fitness equipment and the training of personal fitness trainers from within their department. Chief Altman was particularly proud of the results achieved. "We now have one of the few mandatory fitness programs in the nation for volunteers ... We have gone from a recliner and fried foods model to a ... healthier ... tobacco-free environment," he noted.

The impact of the grant funding was even more spectacular in Rossburg. A small department with a budget of less than $32,500 was able to replace all of their turnout gear and purchase a new, commercial pumper. Chief Coltran stated that, "the Rossburg community is extremely grateful to have received these grants to help protect our community. Without this type of grant we would not have been able to upgrade to this much-needed equipment." The pumper they acquired through the grant replaced a 1960's model.

I saw a picture of these proud individuals decked out in their new gear standing in front of their new pumper. What a proud group of firefighters. What a tremendous tribute to the true intent of the FIRE Act.

As we were leaving town, Jack and I paused to buy some postcards at a downtown store. As we were walking back to my GMC Suburban, we noted a slogan on the DHL company's street pickup container. I like it. See what you think. "The extra mile is part of our regular route." Sounds good to me.

Many thanks to Chief Mark Wolf for sharing the success stories of his department, as well of those of some of his neighbors. The B and B Tour then took off for Fairfield.

Fairfield, Ohio July 11, 2006

Fire Act Allows Department to Expand Their Planned Scope of Service

After taking our leave from Greenville, Jack and I proceeded to take a leisurely drive down U.S. Highway 127. Like many of our nations U.S. highways, U.S. 127 followed a route which wove its way through a variety of different communities. We went many miles without seeing so much as a cross road or a set of traffic signals.

We did encounter a pretty neat traffic control system around a couple of construction sites. Rather than setting out human flaggers and control devices, traffic lights were set up to regulate the traffic on a rotating basis. Each way had the green light for a given period of time. Then the lights went red in both directions. They then turned green for the opposite end. Pretty nifty.

About halfway to our destination of Fairfield, Ohio, the hunger gremlins started dancing around in each of our tummies. I almost lost control of the car because of that one. Once I was able to get the vehicle under control, Jack and I spotted an Arby's restaurant on the side of the road in Eaton, Ohio. We decided to take a trip down memory lane and stop for a roast beef sandwich. It makes a guy feel good to know that some things never change. Yum…

Later in the afternoon we motored into Fairfield. The City of Fairfield is not an older community. As a matter of fact they just celebrated the 50th Anniversary of their incorporation. Apparently fearing an annexation by a neighboring city, the citizens of the community decided to take a hand in their own future and become an incorporated city.

My Yahoo maps are great but they have one shortcoming. Unless you add a specific address to the search, you end up in what they determine to be the geographic center of a community. Rest assured that we were no where near a firehouse when we got to that point.

I called my host and left a message for him to return my call. Jack and I then decided to take in the sights in what turned out to be downtown Fairfield. We turned off of U.S. 127 to explore a large, four-lane local road. As we were observing the shopping centers and a beautiful Catholic church, Jack and I saw what looked like a firehouse on the left side of the road. Sure enough it was Fire Headquarters.

We decided that it would be a great place to wait. As I was turning into the driveway, Captain Russ Kammer returned my call. He said to go on in and that the chief was waiting for us. So in we waltzed. The kindly administrative assistant ushered us in to meet Chief Don Bennett, a veteran of twenty-three years as Chief of the Fairfield Fire Department.

He apologized for an ongoing interview and ushered us into the kitchen for a good cup of firehouse coffee and asked one of his firefighters to give us a tour of the station. What a beautiful building. It was specially built to fit the lot which the city acquired for the station. The entire internal administrative area of the station wraps around a well-appointed training room in the center of the structure.

Maybe it was an architectural fluke and maybe it is a sign of the department's commitment to training as the base of organizational success. Either way, it is a truly functional training area. Upon the return of Captain Kammer from a training assignment, he and the chief sat down with Jack and me to discuss the impact of the grant program on the Fairfield Fire Department.

Before we get into a discussion to FIRE Act grant, let me tell you a few things about this really neat fire department. They are a truly community-focused fire agency. They conduct a bike helmet safety program like none other I have seen. Working with the local Mercy Hospital, Burger King and McDonalds' restaurants, they try to ensure the distribution of bike safety helmets to those who need them. They are ready to provide the youth of the community with a safety helmet if they need one. They are equally able to provide a ticket for a free Happy Meal where the young person is found wearing a proper helmet.

They also have a number of department members who are fully trained to perform child safety seat inspections. Chief Bennett mentioned that they are about to send another six people to the 40-hour training session for this community service program. He also mentioned that during the summer the fire department runs a movies-in-the-park program in the amphitheater behind the station. "People call at the beginning of the summer to get the list of movies for the season," the chief stated.

The chief is also proud of the area Fire Department Chaplaincy Program. After a tragedy a number of years ago, the chief determined that such a program was needed in his region. Starting with a friend who was a local Catholic priest, the Chief has built up a staff of chaplains which includes a number of the younger clergy in the area who have pitched in to make the program a success.

We then moved on to a discussion of the FIRE Act grants which have been received over the past several years. They received grants in 2002, 2004, and 2005. In the first year they created a respiratory protection program which included new self-contained breathing apparatus, fit testing, and the bench testing of equipment.

Their next grant allowed them to acquire three thermal imaging cameras and ten portable radios. Their last grant allowed them to replace the entire inventory of personal protective equipment. Each member was outfitted from head to toe with new gear.

Chief Bennett mentioned the importance of the grant funding when he noted that because of budgetary limitations, none of these items listed above were included in their five-year capital improvement plan. The chief indicated that his original plan was to replace $50,000 of gear every third year. However, he was concerned that he would never catch up because of the dangers of UV degradation.

Perhaps the greatest benefit which came as a result of the infusion of FIRE Act money arises from the fact that the department was able to gain sufficient money from the capital budget to build a new training complex for Captain Kammer's departmental training program.

Money that would have gone for the cameras, radios, turnout gear, and SCBA equipment then became available to build a much-needed training complex. This complex will have a four-story tower and a two-story residential simulator. This is one of the great multiplier effects of the FIRE Act that far too few tout as a reason for increasing the funding for the program to the full $1,000,000,000 level allowed for in the enabling legislation.

The chief is extremely pleased with the increased level of safety which has been afforded to his staff. Better communications and greater operational accountability is now the norm in this department. The added thermal imaging cameras have made the firefighting operations safer and more effective.

This increased level of safety and improved equipment posture has allowed his department to deliver a far higher level of service to the community. He feels that the citizens now receive a far higher level of service since his people are better-trained, well-equipped and highly-motivated.

After the completion of our interview, the Chief was kind enough to present Jack and me with a number of commemorative gifts. I shall cherish them as I use each of them in the future.

The night ended with a traditional firehouse supper created by the troops at Fairfield Station #3. I want to thank Captain Webber and the chef-de-jour Firefighter Chris Theders. The spaghetti and meatballs, salad, and garlic bread were truly scrumptious.

I am so pleased that I was able to meet Chief Don Bennett and his great staff in Fairfield, Ohio. The citizens of that community can rest comfortably knowing this dedicated group is on duty.

Hardinsburg, IN July 12, 2006

The Posey Township Fire Department:
A Lesson in Rural Operations

T oday's journey from Ohio, through Kentucky, and on into Indiana was a stressful one. I guess I can best describe it as a trip through a car wash without the benefit of any soap. Jack and I have not seen any real sun since Saturday. However I want you to know that the farmers out here are really pleased with the rain.

Our stop today was in Hardinsburg, Indiana, a small farming community not far from the Ohio River. Actually Hardinsburg is a small community within the confines of Posey Township, which is located in Washington County. It is an area where major flooding struck a neighboring community to Hardinsburg not too many years ago.

The fire department in that community was wiped out and has not been reestablished. Many people in that community accepted a FEMA buyout of their homes which were all located in a flood plain zone. The blocks of open land where people once lived was really a tough thing to see

The run up U.S. Highway 150 to Posey Township was somewhat akin to traveling a slalom path over a hilly track. My host for this visit was Assistant Chief Dick Doan, a brother Mason and a fellow Past Master of his lodge. His directions to reach his fire station were as simple and folksy as possible. We arrived around 2:00 PM.

At their station, located one block off of U.S. 150, I met with Chief Robert Rippy and his wife Sondra. Mrs. Rippy is an active EMS responder and secretary/treasurer of the Posey Township Volunteer Fire Department. We spent a great deal of time comparing notes and discussing the impact of the FIRE Act.

This is a relatively new fire department, having been formed in 1993. They have two fire stations, one of which is now being used just for storage. The metal clad structure within which we met was built by the firefighters themselves. Mrs. Rippy proudly shared her scrapbook with all of the highlights of their 13 years of service to the township.

Their FIRE Act grants have been a real lifesaver for the department. More than that, they came at a fortunate time for them. In 2001 they received a Community Focus Grant from the State of Indiana to buy a new pumper. The unit that it replaced had originally seen service in Oceanside, NY and came to Posey Township by way about five other fire departments.

Their first grant in 2002 allowed them to purchase 30 full sets of turnout gear. Each member is now equipped, head to toe, with the latest compliant gear. They also received a thermal imaging camera, 17 portable radios, and two mobile radio repeaters. They also received four SCBA units and spare cylinders and face-pieces.

In 2004 their grant allowed them to acquire a wide array of rescue tools and equipment, as well as an exothermic cutting torch and a multi-gas detector. Being really imaginative and inventive people, they converted their older pumper into a rescue vehicle. The hydraulic tools they bought were mated with their existing equipment of the same make and mounted in the rear right side of the hose bed. The tools are mounted right under them and are readily available when needed.

In addition to the rescue equipment, they were able to acquire four more SCBA units with face-pieces and spare cylinders. In addition, they were able to acquire foam system and foam concentrate which they also mounted on their rescue pumper. They now have capabilities which were unimaginable just a few short years ago.

"The grants were a lifesaver for us," Chief Rippy said. "I don't know how we ever would have gotten the money for all of that stuff." Rippy also mentioned me that they had applied for an air compressor unit this year.

The chief also shared a horror story with me about how bad communications are in Washington County. The different departments have a difficult time trying to talk to each other. You have to bear in mind that this is a really rural area, where even cell phone service is somewhat spotty.

The chief managed to acquire a 150-foot radio antenna tower. However he has been unable to get it erected. The concrete pad has been poured, but unfortunately the fellow who was going to help them erect it has not been able to get to the station.

The chief told me about a major fire a few years ago where he had to send one of his pumpers to the top of the hill next to the fire station so that that communications on the hand-held radios could reach the dispatch center. "It was the only way I could think of to get my people talking to one another," the chief candidly stated.

The department is continually looking for new ways to raise funds for the department. Here is a list of fund-raising events that the chief, his wife, and Dick Doan gave me:

- Turkey shoot
- Fish fry
- Demolition derby
- Rodeos
- Mud Drags
- ATV drags
- Mud bog – These are sort of like the mud drags, but the mud is deeper.

My friends, the Posey Township Volunteer Fire Department is expecting more than 40 vehicles to show up for the mud bog they are holding this weekend. Sondra Posey told me that they just cannot give up on their fund raising efforts. Every nickel counts. The latest goal of their fundraising efforts is for an addition to the building so that they can have a real meeting room.

They currently have to pull one of the firefighting units out of the building and take the chairs out of storage to set up for their meetings, which are held at the back of the station. Chief Rippy told me it was his hope that when the new room was built that they would not have to fully heat the whole building, but just the meeting room.

My friends, today's visit was really special for Jack and me. We got to see one of the fire departments in our country for whom the FIRE Act was truly created.

Dana, Indiana July 10, 2006

A Real Special Day for Me

T alk about the Hand of the Lord at work in your life. Today turned out to be a real special day for me. Our travel route through Indiana took us to a location I had never imagined I would ever visit. As I stated in my article describing my Road Trip back in April, the genesis for this trip came from my love for the travel writings of the late Pulitzer-Prize winning war correspondent, Ernie Pyle. I have read and re-read his descriptions of small town America during the 1930's.

Fate came in the form of Randy Vollmer. Randy is the lieutenant who invited me to visit his fire department in Longview, Illinois. The route over U.S. Highway 36 that Yahoo maps created took me right through Ernie Pyle's hometown of Dana, Indiana. I was so pleased to have stumbled across the home of my literary hero.

Jack took pictures of me at the Ernie Pyle Park and in front of the Welcome to Dana, Indiana, Home of Ernie Pyle sign at the entrance to town. Not too far down the road was a sign directing us to the Ernie Pyle historical site in downtown Dana. Jack and I actually got to visit the home where Ernie grew up.

I want to thank Joan and Charity, the historic interpreters for the fine tour of the museum and of the home. A further indicator that the trip to this town was destined to happen comes from the fact that the museum is only open Thursday through Sunday. Wow, what a stroke of luck.

Jack and I signed the visitor's log, watched an introductory movie and wandered among the WWII mementos in the museum. I then proceeded to the gift shop and loaded up on new Ernie Pyle books for my collection. Well new to me anyway. Joan was so impressed with my love for Ernie Pyle that she gave me the gift of an additional book.

After a short stay in an important place, Jack and I pulled up stakes and headed back to the road. By the way, there are some really straight roads out here in Indiana and Illinois.

July 13, 2006 - Longview, Illinois: Population 200

How the Fire Act Windfall Helped the Longview Volunteers Get New Gear

Like I said in my earlier post, July 13 was a really special day for the Harry and Jack road trip. We actually got to see the sun today. As we went wheels up from Corydon, Indiana, Jack and I took off into yet another morning's worth of rain. I am a great fan of the farmers and their need for rain, but enough is enough.

As we motored on past Princeton, Indiana, the rain slowly began to ease up. The sun then burst through the clouds and we were treated to more than 100 miles of beautiful driving through the seemingly endless miles of corn and soybeans. Of course I should add that I saw an absolutely humongous Toyota automobile plant off to the side of the highway in Princeton.

I want you to know that I am gaining a far greater confidence in the agricultural strength of our great nation. Although I come from a place which calls itself the Garden State, I think that the folks in Trenton should turn in their rights to the name. Some of the cornfields out here seem to be as big as the entire state of New Jersey, including the cities.

After many trips to the side of the road to check our maps and directions, we finally managed to make it into the Longview, Illinois Business District. I am not exaggerating when I tell you that there were exactly two stores (one vacant) and the U.S. Post Office in the downtown business district. There are, however, a passel of neatly arranged homes covering about nine very small blocks.

As Jack and I sat taking the air, our host Randy Vollmer called us to tell us he was delayed at his job teaching CPR at the Illinois Fire Service Institute at the University of Illinois complex in south Champaign. He asked if we would like to visit the site. Jack and I quickly agreed and, after jotting down some cryptic directions, headed off to Champaign, about 20 miles north of Longview.

Randy greeted us and took us in to meet Brian Bauer, head of the firefighting program at the Institute. What a tremendous facility. After discussing the manner in which courses are delivered all across the state. Brian took us outside for the full tour of the facility. I was fortunate enough to be able to watch a recruit class from the Chicago Fire Department going through its paces in a variety of smoke-house evolutions.

Jack and I were really impressed with the manner in which the site had been laid out to cover a wide range of training courses. There was an entire area devoted to collapse rescue. There were more than a dozen specially-laid-out props where parallel tunnels were created, one with obstructions and one for the instructors to monitor the evolution.

There was also a specially built three-story structure made out of inter-modal containers that is used for confined-space entry, rappelling, elevator rescue, and ladder-raising evolutions. There are also mock elevators which are used for rescue operations from stuck elevators. In another are of the facility, we saw a relatively inexpensive burn building created from metal shipping containers. These have been duplicated in a series of relatively inexpensive burn buildings which have been built in a variety of locations around the state.

Since the facility is so large, Brian was chauffeuring us around in a very neat three-seat golf cart-like cart. As we halted to check another group of Chicago fire cadets, the institute director Richard Jaehne came coasting up beside us in a similar mobile transportation cart.

My friends, Dick Jaehne is as forceful and effective an advocate for the fire service and fire training as any man I have ever met. However, I would expect nothing less from a retired Marine Colonel and a holder of the Navy Cross for heroism in action during the Vietnam War. I have worked with the Colonel on a number of occasions and know him to be one of the top people in our field.

After bidding adieu to Colonel Jaehne and Brian Bauer, Jack and I returned to Longview with Randy. When we arrived, the firehouse was open and ready for inspection, with all of the units lined up out front. I should point out from the get-go that both the pumper and the tanker were well over 25 years old. Randy mentioned that they were trying to raise funds to get new equipment, but were having little success.

They also have a 1991 heavy rescue vehicle which was purchased second hand a number of years ago. They cover a fairly large highway area within their fire district. They also provide fire protection and rescue services for the neighboring community of Broadlands.

During my interviews with the newspaper folks from Champaign/Urbana, the photographer candidly told me that this was only the second time in 18 years at the paper when he had been in Longview. He attributed this to the fact that the people get along so well there. He said that there were no hissy fits in government to cover because everyone got along so well out in Longview.

I would also like to report to you that the interviews which I had with the local ABC affiliate TV-3 led off the late news on local television in the Champaign/Urbana, Decatur, and Danville areas. The station was extremely creative, in that it tied our story into the Champaign County Fire Chief's monthly meeting where the new equipment, from Urbana, which was partly acquired with FIRE Act funding, was introduced to the county fire service.

I spent a couple of hours talking with the gang in the back room at the Longview Fire Station. Sitting in with us were Mikal Sutton-Vereen of Senator Barack Obama's Springfield office and Brian Kelly of Congressman Timothy V. Johnson's Champaign office. They were genuinely interested in the story that all of us had to tell. They both assured me that they would make my views known to the Senator and the Congressman. I thanked them for taking the time to come out to be with us.

After taking our leave from Longview, we motored over to Champaign to rest our weary heads. Tomorrow, we are off to visit Goose Lake, Iowa, next stop on the B and B tour of America.

Goose Lake, Iowa July 15, 2006

✳

The Great Goose Lake, Iowa Meeting
of the Minds

Today was another great day. It all started when we were finally able to leave the Bates Motel in downtown Champaign, Illinois. I will not name the chain where we stayed, but it is possible that Franklin Roosevelt stayed there on one of his many cross-country railroad trips. Jack and I were also treated to another beautiful, sunny day in the Midwestern part of our great nation.

If there is any doubt as to the future of ethanol-based fuels for our country, you folks need only come out to the corn-belt areas where we have traveled the last few days. There are even signs by the side of the road which are laid out like the Burma Shave signs of a long-gone era. Each has a message that ends up with words that urge passing motorist to support the ethanol fuel effort or ask them to think soy-based, bio-diesel.

Many miles down the road, hunger began to creep into our souls. Lunch time found us in Galesburg, Illinois. After gassing up our GMC chariot, we headed south to the business district in search of those famous Golden Arches. Many were the signs which reminded Jack and me that we were in the birthplace of famous poet Carl Sandburg.

Rest assured that I am not now motivated to create a stirring sonnet based upon well-placed iambic pentameter rhymes. The only poetry which came to my mind involved a young man from Nantucket. We will leave it at that.

The run from Galesburg to the Mississippi River Bridge on Interstate 80 took a little less than an hour. Fortunately Jack was feeding me the travel directions one after the other because our exit to U.S. Highway 67 north was only about ¼ mile from the base of the bridge. The route north ran right along the Mississippi for about six miles past Le Clare and on toward Clinton.

As we moved north, we passed through a number of neat small communities. As we entered the response area of the Low Moor Volunteer Fire Department, we noted their personnel operating by the side of the highway. There was also a remote truck on-scene from an area television station, as well as cruisers from the local sheriff's office.

Sadly, we later learned that they were conducting a search and recovery operation for a drowning victim. As usual the fire service was out on location doing their duty, just like fire departments all across the nation. Sometimes we experience joy and sometimes we are a part of stark tragedy.

A little bit further up the highway, we came to a fork in the road where our instincts told us to go one way and the directions were a bit unclear about the other road. Since confusion was clouding our vision, Jack and I pulled to the side of the road to reboot our mental directional computers. At just about the same time that our minds came back on line, my cell phone rang. Thankfully it was our host Paul Doyle, the training officer for the Goose Lake Volunteer Fire Department.

He provided a great set of corrections to the directions. I believe they were something along the lines of "head on up the road about 15 miles and make a left at the large white windmill. Then go about two miles up the road and make a right on to Main Street. Go up to the first stop sign and then turn right at the bank."

We did exactly as directed and found ourselves headed right for the city hall/fire station. We were in downtown Goose Lake, population 232. The department's newest (and only) pumper was parked out on the apron of the station. Paul and his Chief, Kevin Cain came striding down the ramp to welcome us to their community.

They escorted us into the station's air-conditioned combination kitchen, radio room and office, so that we could chat in comfort. A short time later, Steve Farrell, another member of the department came in to meet with us. As Jack and I were setting up to begin the interview, Chief Cain began taking goodies out of the icebox. It seemed like and endless stream of cookies and brownies, interspersed with cans of pop. So much for my Atkins diet.

Goose Lake was an interesting addition to our Road Trip. These fine folks have not yet received a FIRE Act grant. They are 0 for three tries at bat. Jack and I wanted to find out what they needed and how they felt about their situation.

Let me tell you a little bit about what we discovered. The Goose Lake Volunteer Fire Department was founded in 1915. This was only a couple of years after the city was appropriated in 1912. Their annual budget is only $5,000 dollars. The metal fire station where we met was built by the fire department members themselves.

While the city insures their vehicles, all other expenses must be met out of the $5,000 figure. They estimated that about $2,000 of their budget went to repairs on the vehicles each year. Their fleet consists of a 1984 pumper, a 1,000 tanker they built themselves, and a very old grass firefighting vehicle. They supplement their budget with an annual fire department supper.

The current pumper replaced a 1974 model that was always in danger of not starting or not returning from a run. They were most fortunate, in that a local chemical company donated the 1984 pumper to them when a newer unit arrived. Chief Cain told me that there was no way that they could have afforded a better pumper out of their existing budgetary resources.

"We are tickled to death to have the 22-year-old pumper that was donated to us by the Lyondell/Equistar company. It beats the daylights out of what we had," Chief Cain told me. "Our old 1974 pumper was getting to be am expensive maintenance problem."

They built the tanker themselves. They received a surplus chassis on loan from the government. A local company donated a 1,000-gallon tank to them that they were going to scrap. It cost them $200 to buy the frame to mount the tank on the chassis. Their grass firefighting vehicle is also a surplus vehicle on loan from the government.

Their turnout gear was purchased over the course of a number of years in the early 1990's. They have a grand total of five self-contained breathing apparatus units in service. There are a number of other SCBA units which are not currently useable because the tanks are obsolete.

During the past year they responded to 35 runs. Some runs were in the one-square mile city, but most were mutual aid calls to surrounding communities. All five of the fires they responded to were in mutual aid communities. They are on automatic response with one nearby community and are part of a mutual aid agreement with all of the other communities in Clinton County.

Most of their runs out of town are in the 10-15 mile range. This can lead to problems as the 1984 pumper has only a two-man cab. Chief Cain said that they try to put a third person in the cab whenever they can. Sometimes members have to ride the back step because there is no where else to ride. Many times members follow the pumper in their own cars or respond in the brush truck.

Goose Lake has the school district's new consolidated K-12 school in the city. It is about a block from the fire station. When the school is in session Chief Cain estimates that the population of the community rises to well over 1,000 people, students and faculty alike.

The school is a designated evacuation site for the northern part of Clinton County in the Cordova Nuclear Plant's existing evacuation plan. The department is one of the fire agencies designated to set up a large decontamination site in the event of an incident. They are expected to handle more than 20,000 people on site. Think about that one for awhile.

About an hour into our meeting, Randy Novak, Chief of the Iowa Fire Service Training Bureau arrived. He had driven over 3-1/2 hours from his office in Ames to be with us. He joined us to discuss the issue of fire service training in his state.

Iowa has the oldest statewide training program in the nation. They have also established a working partnership with 15 area community colleges throughout the state that allows for classes to be taught in all parts of the state. They have a number of mobile units which respond throughout the state to allow for a variety of courses to be taught in the areas where the students live.

The State of Iowa certifies fire personnel to eleven different levels under the IFSAC accreditation program. Very shortly they will be accredited to certify individuals under the Pro Board System. Novak takes pride in the fact that soon personnel in the state will receive joint accreditation under the two different nationally-recognized fire training certification programs

Jack and I also got to meet Andy McGovern, Training Officer of the Clinton, Iowa Fire Department. He arrived at about the same time as Randy. He shared the fact that Clinton had received FIRE Act grants in four of the last five years. With their funds, they were able to add ventilation systems to all three of their stations. They also received new turnout gear for all 44 of their personnel.

In addition they now have a mandatory fitness program based upon the fitness equipment they received under the act. They also received specialized rescue equipment and emergency generators for all of their stations.

We were also fortunate to have Alison Hart from Senator Tom Harkin's Davenport office stop by in Goose Lake. She indicated the Senator's strong, long-time support for the FIRE Act. We then took turns answering a variety of questions from Ms. Hart on my road trip, the state of fire training in Iowa, and the need to increase the level of funding appropriations for the FIRE Act.

She was most pleased to hear of the Fire Service Training Bureau's statewide support effort for the FIRE Act. Randy mentioned to her that his office helps fire departments across the state by reviewing their grant application narratives. He also mentioned that he is able to use the state's satellite up-link system to provide state-wide training on how to fill out the grant applications.

"Our firefighters are getting better at writing the narratives," Randy mentioned. "Where I would review more than 150 application narratives in years past, there were only about 55 this year."

Our stop in Goose Lake was an extremely important addition to the data base Jack and I are gathering on our road trip. Jack and I got the word about our road trip to Ms. Hart. Goose Lake got to tell their story to the world. I got to learn a great deal about the outstanding training efforts of Randy Novak and the fine folks at the Iowa Fire Service Training Bureau. And I got to meet Andy McGovern from the Clinton, Iowa Fire Department. What a great day.

Jack and I were also most fortunate to be able to follow Andy to our motel in Clinton. Following him rather than my Yahoo Map directions saved us several miles of travel. Tomorrow it is on to Glenville, Minnesota.

Glenville, Minnesota July 15, 2006

We Have Seen the Future

Life can be a real hoot. You just never know what you might learn on any given day. There is always something new out there. Today was no different. Not long after leaving Clinton, Iowa for our next stop in Glenville, Minnesota, we saw signs which indicated that we were about to pass near to the World's Largest Truck Stop.

So what you might say. Can you imagine how many truck stops Jack and I have seen over the course of our last ten days on the road. Let me assure you that there has been more then one my friends, more than one. So we were curious as we moved west on Interstate 80.

Not too far down the road we passed by the Iowa 80 Truck Stop in Wolcott, Iowa. Jack and I saw little to dispute their claim to the title. They have space for nearly 900 tractor-trailers in their parking area. They also have their own movie theater, a wireless Internet area, a dentist, and a barbershop. Not too mention food, showers, and diesel fuel.

They now have a multi-million dollar expansion underway. This month, a 17,000 square-foot SuperTruck showroom featuring a yellow Peterbilt 379 semitrailer on a lighted turntable and a wall filled with truck accessory lights will be added to the "World's Largest Truckstop." I must say that we were impressed with what we saw as I slowed down the "grey ghost" to take a peek.

For the past several days Jack and I have been traveling through states where it would appear that raising corn and soy beans is a great part of their economy. We have also seen a tremendous number of advertisements along the sides of the roads touting the bio-diesel and ethanol fuel industry. Today Jack and I met the future of alternatives fuels in a small town in Southern Minnesota.

Just before we crossed from Iowa into Minnesota Jack and I saw our first E-85 ethanol fill station advertising by the side of the road. There is also an E-85 station located near our hotel room in Austin, Minnesota. Anyway, our journey into Glenville thrust us into the future.

Glenville is a small community of approximately 800 folks located about six miles off of Interstate 35 in the southeastern part of Minnesota. It is located within Freeborn County which has a population of approximately 35,000. It is also about 15 miles west of Austin where one of my favorite food products is made. I am referring of course to the inimitable SPAM; the food, not the Internet nuisance. Jack and I were going to take in the SPAM museum, but it was closed by the time we got there.

Anyway, when we arrived in town, it was easy to find the building where the fire trucks were. There was a red rescue unit parked out front of a metal garage. It seems that the town is in the midst of building a new station about 100 yards up the street. Our host, Lt. Matt Webb was out front to great us. He apologized for the lack of a crowd, but told me that the members would be there as soon as he toned out my arrival on the dispatch system. Among the people who came out was Wes Webb, Matt's father, a fellow firefighter, and Mayor of Glenville.

The fire department's four-vehicle fleet has been stored in the municipal public works building during the construction period. In addition to the rescue vehicle, there is a 1989 pumper, a 1994 tanker with a 3,000 gallon tank and two portable drop tanks, and a 1974 brush firefighting vehicle. The tanker and the pumper were both pre-owned units, as our friends in the used car business are so fond of saying.

The FIRE Act grant they received in 2005 allowed them to outfit their entire department from head-to-toe with brand new gear. They also were able to purchase 20 new self-contained breathing apparatus units with an additional 26 spare cylinders.

In speaking with the members of the department who came out to visit with us, it became obvious that they are really pleased with their new gear. More than one person spoke of the ease of donning and the comfort that went along with using their new gear. One man even mentioned that he had not had a single blister since receiving his new leather boots.

During our discussions it was mentioned that all of the turnout gear and SCBA that was replaced by the FIRE Act acquisitions went to a nearby mutual aid fire department. The members thought that the Mayor was joking with them when he called to offer all of the surplus gear to them.

When they finally came to understand that he was serious, they loaded up on five pickup trucks and zipped right on over to Glenville. Wes Webb told us that they couldn't stop smiling as they drove back to their community with their "new-to-them" gear. My friends, this is an added side benefit to the FIRE Act. Many times the equipment being replaced can be given to another department which has a need for that gear. This is a very good thing.

During our discussions, the Mayor mentioned the two

newest industries in town. There is an ethanol manufacturing plant, as well as a bio-diesel plant which adjoins the ethanol facility. Mayor Webb told us that the ethanol facility is capable of manufacturing 35 million gallons of product per year. Ethanol is the basis for the E-85 alternative fuel that is being touted as one way to relieve our dependence on foreign fuel sources. The bio-diesel plant has a 24 million gallon manufacturing capacity. He mentioned that each facility also had approximately one million gallons of product on site at any given time.

The bulk ingredients arrive at the plants by both road and rail. A new siding has been built to accommodate the increased needs of this burgeoning industry. The finished products depart in a similar manner. At any time, thousands of gallons of alternative fuels are moving in and out of this lovely rural community.

Glenville and their surrounding neighbors in Freeborn County are in the forefront of an industry that will be coming to a town near you in the not too distant future.

The fire department has a stock of approximately 70 five-gallon containers of alcohol foam. There is a great deal more that they will have to acquire to improve their capabilities with these new hazardous materials.

Let me tell you that we also saw a wide variety of new grain storage and silo facilities in both Minnesota and Iowa. Tom Harkin, one of the two U.S. Senators from Iowa, (and a possible candidate for President), has made it his mission to make Iowa a leader in the alternative fuel industry.

We were only about ten miles over the border into Minnesota when we saw the new Glenville facilities. These plants are going to be built in rural areas, near the source of their raw materials. I can only imagine the challenges which lie just around the corner for our rural fire service brethren in the coming years. We are surely going to need more than the FIRE Act to cope with this new industry.

A crew arrived from local television station TV-6 not long after our discussions began to slow down. Once again I was interviewed about the reasons for my road trip and the needs of the American Fire Service. I took pains to stress the need for people to contact their Senators and Members of Congress to ask for support in bumping up the appropriations to the full maximum of one billion dollars.

After taking the time to speak with all of the members in attendance, and shake hands all around Jack and I took our leave. As we moved down the road toward Austin, Jack and I chatted back and forth about how we had seen the future. We spoke about how major facilities like this would begin to pop up all over the country. I think that we have truly seen the future of fuel in our nation. Are you ready to fight fires in the new alcohol-based products?

After a good night's sleep B and B will be heading toward Wisconsin. Take care and stay safe.

Wyocena, Wisconsin July 15, 2006

We Actually See Our First New Fire Truck

Another new day dawned in the upper Midwest today. Like the last several days we have seen, it looked to be another really hot and sunny day. As we stepped out of the motel to head for breakfast, it was 86 degrees at 0830 hr. Unlike yesterday, there was no breeze to agitate the air.

Since supper was so good in the restaurant next to our motel last night, we returned for a repeat performance. It was here that the lovely Heather made my day. After the hostess gave us our coffee and water Heather stopped by our table to take our order.

She looked at me liked she knew me. She paused to ponder a moment and then said, "didn't I see you on television last night? You were talking about the federal government helping the fire department up in Glenville." Yes, I said, that was me. She told me that it was real neat and then proceeded to take our order.

Talk about working your way into my heart. She could do no wrong in my eyes after that point. Of course I ordered the over-55 special to save a couple of bucks. What's the sense of getting older if you can't use it from time to time to save a buck?

Our trip over to Wyocena went quite well. The Yahoo map directions were fairly simple. They said to turn right on Interstate 90 and go 217.3 miles. I quickly discovered why the trip time was listed at only three hours and forty minutes. The speed limit was 70 miles-per-hour and being a good citizen I went the limit.

However, after almost ending up as a hood ornament on an eastbound tractor-trailer I stepped it up just a bit. It was my intention not to meet a member of the Minnesota or Wisconsin state law enforcement community. I don't know, maybe it's just me, but it was more than a little embarrassing getting passed by a number of elderly ladies. Maybe things are different out here in this part of the country. Anyway Jack and I made great time and saw only one police vehicle in 217.3 miles of driving.

Wyocena is a small Wisconsin farming community, population 717, located about 30 miles north of the state capitol in Madison. There are a number of small businesses in town, as well as a cheese factory (it is Wisconsin after all), a county highway maintenance facility, and resident health care facility.

Our host, Assistant Chief Don Catannaci was waiting for us outside of the community's small, one-story, metal fire station. The sign on the door proudly proclaimed that I had arrived at the Wyoncena Bureau of Fire's Station No. 1. When asked, Don owned up to the fact that there was no Station #2.

During our visit we also met Chief Jared Anderson and Firefighter Brian Lemanczyk. They had taken a break from building a deck on the home of the chief's father. I should point out that the temperature at the time was about 97 degrees, so that it was not a hard decision for them to stop by and chat for awhile in their air conditioned meeting room.

After the interview, Jack and I went outside to take a look at the new pumper which the department had received as a result of their 2005 FIRE Act grant. It had only recently arrived and was not yet in service. Don told me that they were still waiting for a few final items that needed to be installed before the unit could go into service.

They have spent a number of evenings learning how to drive and operate their new pumper. When all of the equipment has been installed and the members familiarized with it use, the unit will go into active service.

They also received a number of new self-contained breathing apparatus units as a result of their 2003 FIRE Act grant. Along with that they got several spare cylinders, and a SEMS system, as well as a laptop computer to assist them in maintaining their new accountability system. "Once our SEMS is fully in service, it will provide us with a more efficient way of monitoring our firefighters during firefighting operations," Chief Catenacci said.

An air compressor refill station also came in to the department from the same grant. The department has been able to increase the level of their SCBA training. They no longer have to travel to a neighboring department to refill their cylinders. "The light-weight and more ergonomic back-frame has made using the air packs more comfortable," the chief noted.

Don went on how to describe how a number of the area fire units worked together in creating their grant applications and narratives. They looked at what made up the successful grant packages. "You need to see what successful grant recipients have done to guide your efforts," Catenacci stated. "You do not copy what they did, but you can see how they put their case together."

As Don and I chatted after the real interview period was at an end, I discovered that he and I have something really neat in common. Both he and I are living in the homes where our wives grew up. I think that is real special. The roots for each of us run deep indeed.

After thanking Don for the invitation and having him check our travel directions to Madison, we took our leave of Wyocena, Wisconsin.

Monroe, Wisconsin July 17, 2006

We Made Our First Emergency Response

Last night was laundry night for Jack and me in Madison, Wisconsin. You can only imagine how many washers and dryers that people our size have to use. Since our hotel did not have a washer and dryer (the first so far in this chain), we were sent about five minutes up the street. It was time to cleanse our extra clothes.

Let me share one important lesson with you. When the temperature is in the low 90's, try to find a laundry facility where the air conditioning is working. It was hard to tell whether it was the heat from the street or the heat from the dryers which was the cause of our sweating festival. Once our job was completed, we swiftly returned to the air conditioned comfort of our hotel room.

Since we were not that far from our next stop in Monroe, we treated ourselves to a late wakeup call and another great Hampton Inn free breakfast. Let me tell you my friends, the three nights which we spent in other chain motels convinced me that Hampton Inns will be my destination of choice whenever possible.

We hit the road at about 1100 hrs. Once again we checked with the kindly young lady at the front desk to be sure that we were heading the right way. Since she was familiar with the area she was able to shave a few miles off of the trip. She was a good source of information.

Let me share a short traffic story with you. After my journey around Madison, the state capitol of Wisconsin, I am willing to stack up the traffic here against any city, except maybe New York or Boston. Heavy traffic kept moving on and off of the highway. It was tough. However, after all was said and done, this turned out to be one of our shortest legs of the journey at only 54 miles. Heck, the "grey ghost" was hardly warmed up by the time we got to Monroe.

I might not be from Wisconsin, but I sure do love my cheese. I cannot tell you how many times I have experienced the joy of cutting cheese. Monroe is the home of the last plant in the United States that makes limburger cheese. Were we closer to the end of the trip, I might have purchased some. However, I do not think the cheese would fare too well over the course of the next three weeks until we get home.

Our host for the day was Fire Chief Daryl Rausch. I was pleased to note that Chief Rausch is a brother Mason. We exchanged a variety of stories about the craft as we discussed the fire department and their success with the FIRE Act grant process.

Our trip to Monroe was truly enlightening and exciting. I would rate it second only to the Great Hershey Train Wreck in terms of excitement and enlightenment. Monroe is a smaller regional center. As I was interviewing Chief Rausch for my road trip journal the tones went off for a reported fire at a manufacturing plant on the west end of town. Battalion Chief Lane Heins had arrived before the chief and established command on the A/B side of the structure. Chief Rausch left Lane in charge and assumed the sector command for the C side of the building.

Over the course of the next hour, I got to see a number of things in use that were acquired thanks to the largess of the FIRE Act. It actually started before we left the fire station. Thanks to the grant funding, there are on-board computers on each of the first alarm units. As the chief's vehicle was warming up, he keyed in the address of the structure where the fire was reported and was pulling up the pre-incident planning data en route to the location.

During the course of the operation, I also got to see their new turnout gear and self-contained breathing apparatus in use as the responding units began to arrive and deploy. The response to the incident included three pumpers, two command units, and an aerial tower. Astoundingly the personnel response during a weekday afternoon was phenomenal. Counting the two chiefs, a total of twenty-nine people were at this alarm.

Perhaps it is important to note that Monroe maintains a paid-on-call firefighting force. The two chiefs are the only full-time staff. Over the years the fire department has built up a fabulous working relationship with a number of firms in the community. These companies allow their people to respond at any time. Chief Rausch mentioned that some of the companies even maintain special firefighter's parking so that department members can easily leave for fire calls. He is most pleased with the manner in which the department and the community interact.

The city has a population of approximately 11,000. There are a number of industrial and agricultural firms doing business in the city. Jack and I saw a great deal of growth coming to the community. Their first-in-the-state Wal-Mart is being replaced by a new Superstore in the coming months.

They also have a major ethanol production plant out on the

west side of their community. There is even a modern alternative fuels station located outside of the plant gate that offers varying blends of product from E-10 to E-85. The difference in price was significant in deed. The E-85 was being sold at $2.16 per gallon and the E-10 at $3.01.

Like Jack and I have been saying my friends, alternative fuels are going to spread east and west from the Midwest. Chief Rausch told us that the plant is selling so much ethanol that they do not have time to add fuel to their on-site storage tanks. The plant is in operation on a 24/7 basis and only shuts down four days a year for maintenance. The company even solicited the help of the fire department and is a good corporate neighbor according to the chief.

We also saw something that will warm the heart of my buddy Billy Goldfeder. As each unit rolled in on the response we noted that every member was riding seated and belted. When asked about this, the chief told me that their policy in this area is strict indeed. If a person is seen without a seatbelt, that member, the driver, and the officer on the rig will all face the music together. "We are pretty close to 100 percent compliance," Chief Rausch proudly stated.

During our discussions, the chief mentioned that they have an extremely close working relationship with Tammy Brown, their district Member of The U.S. Congress. The folks in Monroe know that it will take continuing close interaction to keep the issue of FIRE Act funding in the forefront of Ms. Brown's agenda.

"We have work hard to get the FIRE Act up to its full funding level of one-billion dollars," Chief Rausch stated. The chief also urged me to carry the message across the nation that we need to keep the current peer review process in place.

Chief Rausch went on to explain that there is a fabulous level of support in the community for their fire department. The department was able to acquire a fire safety house and a new

ATV and trailer for off road operations thanks to the generosity of the citizens of Monroe. "B/C Lane delivers more than 200 educational classes in the community each year," Chief Rausch proudly noted.

After a nice lunch at a local German restaurant we took our leave of this lovely little gem in the southern tier of Wisconsin.

Cedarburg, Wisconsin July 18, 2006

The Home of Big League Fund-Raising

After several days of really hot, terrible weather, Jack and I (along with the whole state of Wisconsin) got relief from the oppressive heat this morning. It was about 101 degrees yesterday, and a little hotter the day before. Today the thermometer topped out at about 82 degrees, with a gentle breeze.

As Jack and I traveled up Wisconsin Route 26 toward Interstate 94, we started discussing a friend who is serving on active duty with the U.S. Air Force in Baghdad. His name is John "Mitch" Mitchell and he is a member of the Berlin, Massachusetts Fire Department, where Jack is the safety officer. He is a Massachusetts Air National Guard staff sergeant and serves as a crash-rescue firefighter.

I asked Jack if he thought that Mitch was keeping up with our road trip over in the war zone. Jack called his wife Sue, who works at the Massachusetts Firefighting Academy to ask if she knew or not. Before asking whether he was or not, Sue told Jack that the air conditioning had died this morning and that the temperature was spiraling upward. Being the good husband that he is, he did not mention anything about our weather good fortune. Then Sue confirmed that Mitch was indeed following our progress.

Getting to Cedarburg involved taking a long end run around a major downtown Milwaukee construction project. Jack and I finally caught up with Interstate 43 and struck out northward. It was interesting to note that the Wisconsin landscape changed from urban, to suburban, to rural in very short order.

As we turned onto Washington Avenue in Cedarburg, we were treated to a beautiful slice of old time, Norman Rockwell, small town America. The pace of life seemed to be unhurried and the architecture quite beautiful. Our route to the fire station on Mequon Road took us over a lovely bridge with the quiet waters of the Cedar Creek moving over the town damn.

Cedarburg is a town of 17,250 citizens who live within its 33 square mile area. The economic outlook is quite stable and they have a wide array of retail, residential, commercial, and manufacturing occupancies in their town. There were also a number of stylish antique shops.

The fire station was a combination of a variety of architectural styles dating back to the early 20th Century. As a matter of fact, one part of the station, which now serves as the support facility/museum, once served as the town's police station. The word Jail was engraved over the arched door which once led to the community lock-up. They have two stations as well as the support facility/museum.

I would like to point out early on that Cedarburg has an outstanding array of antique fire apparatus. They have the first two pumpers they ever owned, a 1924 Graham, and a 1927 Pirsch. They also have their 1957 FWD rear-mount aerial ladder. In their meeting rooms they have the most complete set of fire extinguishers on display that I have ever seen. It was donated by a citizen and contains fire extinguishers manufactured between 1850 and 1950.

We met with our host, Training Officer Mike LaRosa, who was waiting for us in front of their new station next to the old. He introduced us to Fire Chief Richard Van Dinter and Engineer Thomas Marquardt, Director of Public Works for the Town.

We toured the station and examined the equipment which they received from their FIRE Act grants in 2004 and 2005. The first grant allowed them to purchase sufficient portable radios for every riding position on their first alarm vehicles. Their 2005 grant allowed them to upgrade their existing self-contained breathing apparatus units.

It also provided an SCBA fill station, RIT packs, and training materials. I would like you to note that they upgraded their existing units rather than going for new models. This is an excellent example of how to stretch the use of the FIRE Act funding.

My friends, these folks have created one of the most ingenious on-site drill grounds that I have ever seen. What once served as the town water tank, behind the old police station has been transformed into an interesting fire training ground. They first had to completely sandblast the interior of the tank to clean off the tar sealer. The chief mentioned that he was shaking sand out of this hair for days after this task was completed.

Inside of the tank they created a multi-level series of mockups. There was a residential living area, complete with furniture, as well as an entanglement obstacle with many different ways to snag the unwary firefighter. They also created a mockup that allows them to hang drywall in order to conduct breaching exercises.

Mike La Rose mentioned that the area fills up quite quickly with the artificial smoke that they use. Jack and looked at each other and agreed that once the main door was closed, it must be as dark as the inside of tomb in there. They can conduct year-round training even during the worst that a Wisconsin winter can throw at them.

Chief Van Dinter took great pains to explain that not one piece of their excellent apparatus fleet was purchased with municipal funding. They raised all of the money to buy the four engines, one tower ladder, one heavy rescue, two 2 BLS units, two grass rigs, and two support vehicles.

When asked how they were able to do this, the chief mentioned that they conducted four quarterly Maxwell Day flea markets at the Cedarburg Fireman's Field. The fire department owns a 19-acre complex not far from the center of town. It was purchased by them in 1940 and over the years has seen motorcycle racing, car racing, and harness racing serve as departmental fund-raisers. Now it serves as the base for their fund-raising efforts. The chief also took pains to point out that their fiscal policies were conservative. They only buy when they can afford to.

We visited their new second station out on the north side of the town. They created a lovely new brick structure that has a special classic look about it. It was built on land donated by a neighboring airport, and was constructed in a way that allows it to blend in with older brick structures in the area.

In the case of the Cedarburg Fire Department it was the FIRE Act money which allowed them to acquire equipment that could not have been purchased or upgraded for a number of years. After saying good bye to Chief Van Dinter, Mike La Rosa, and Tom Marquart, we made our way back to Interstate 43 and began our not-so-lengthy drive to our next stop in Cudahy.

*New Turnout Gear for W.R. Castle Fire Company
Wittensville, KY.*

*The old home-made 1975 pumper and the new
FIRE Act funded pumper.*

The new Fire Act-funded pumper in Gilt Edge, Tennessee.

Jack Peltier

Posey Township Volunteer Fire Department, Hardinsburg, Indiana (L-R Asst Chief Richard Doan, Carter, Secretary/Treasurer Sondra Rippy, and Chief Robert Rippy).

Johnstown, Pennsylvania High-Tech Communication's Unit.

Lt. Rodney Sonderman of the Hershey, Pennsylvania Fire Department shows the author one of the new computers purchased with FIRE Act funding.

Cudahy, Wisconsin July 18, 2006

Home of One of My Favorite Foods

Have you ever noted how much of a person's life revolves around food? Heaven knows that a great deal of my life has revolved around food in one way or another. But I guess one look at me would tell you that I am not the product of a starving home. I guess you might say the same thing about my buddy Jack Peltier. Both of us serve as a stark testimony to the impact of carbohydrates on the human body. Luckily, we rent out by the pound, so it works to our advantage.

I kept wondering why the name Cudahy seemed to mean something to me. It became quite obvious during discussions with our host Mark Siggelkow and Fire Chief Richard Demien and Commander Gary Posda. It turns out that Cudahy, Wisconsin takes its name from the Cudahy family, and the Patrick Cudahy Company, one of the world's large pork processing firms.

Jack and I were seated in Cudahy Station #2, less than a mile from the plant that makes the fabulous bacon which I love to eat. Maybe you know the kind I like, the kind where you microwave it for about 40 seconds, and voila, instant BLT. If you like bacon bits, chances are great that they too come from this same plant.

Not far from the Cudahy plant you will find the Ladish Corporation, one of the major aerospace contractors in the world. Mark told us that if something has gone into space, chances are good that part of it was made in Cudahy. Ace World Wide, the primary area of inter-modal shipping and international trade for the Port of Milwaukee is also located in Cudahy. They are a city on the way up.

It should be noted that the Cudahy Fire Department predates the founding of the city by a number of years. It began in 1902 as a volunteer fire department and in the late 1960's became a full-time career department. Major rail lines bisect the city and after a number of fatal fires occurred, where responses were delayed by the train lines, it was decided that a second station was needed.

The department provides fire and BLS ambulance service to this industrial city of 18,500 living within the 4.5 square miles of the community. They participate in an extensive mutual aid agreement with the other fire departments of the Milwaukee County area. They also have a strong mutual aid relationship with the U.S. Air Force Reserve base located at the nearby General Mitchell Airport.

Sadly, all of the area departments are going to lose the strong back-up support of the Air Reserve Base, as it has been slated for closing by the Federal Base Realignment Commission (BRAC). Like small departments all around the nation who look to their military neighbors for support, Cudahy will now have to look elsewhere for their help. We are facing the same issue at home with the closing of Fort Monmouth in New Jersey. I sometimes wonder what is on the minds of the people who make these decisions.

We examined the FIRE Act funded items received by the department. They received new SCBA, and an air-refill compressor and station, a station-mounted vehicle exhaust system for both stations, washer/extractor equipment to keep their turnout gear clean, and a full set of fitness equipment and training to use it properly.

The department now has a mandatory physical fitness program. Mark told Jack and me that the new program, when combined with department physicals is paying great dividends. Please note that the physicals were not a part of the FIRE Act funding.

Mark mentioned to me that the addition of the air compressor and fill station has allowed them to conduct more of their SCBA drills on tank air. It is better and more realistic than it was in the past. The FIRE Act grant provided SCBA to replace units that were more than twenty years old. "It was constantly failing and in many cases, beyond repair," Mark told us. In addition, the city had to rent air tanks with which to fill the SCBA cylinders. It is much better now.

Chief Demien told us that his members are now able to provide a better service to the citizens of Cudahy. They are in much better shape, and possess far more confidence in their breathing apparatus. They are also healthier because they are no longer breathing diesel emissions in the station. The FIRE Act has allowed for the creation of an all-around better operation.

Chief Demien and Mark Siggelkow both urged me to take forward the message that the peer-review process must be maintained and that the funding level must be raised to the one billion dollar authorized level. They are pleased with the results which Cudahy has achieved. They are now better able to fulfill their federal role as a primary response agency to assist the 128th Air National Guard Wing at the Airport in mass casualty operations.

Another FIRE Act success story to be sure. After a good night's rest B and B are headed for their next stop in Illinois.

July 18, 2006

Special Update for Posey Township Volunteer Fire Company

My friends, I received a truly great email this evening. I have put off writing my blog entries for Cedarburg and Cudahy, Wisconsin this evening for a few moments to report on a wonderful happenstance which just occurred. I just received an email from Chief Blake Bowers of the Lanton Volunteer Fire Department in West Plains, Missouri. Let me share that email with you. I hope you will be as moved as I was.

Harry,

I have read some of your Blog - and was interested in the Posey Township situation.

As a tower company, as well as being very dedicated to our own rural Fire Department (I am the Chief, and my son and co-worker is one of the Assistant Chiefs,) I think I may be able to help them out, either helping them to put up their existing tower, or possibly putting up a larger tower on a cooperative deal.

Either way, it would be at no cost to them if they have all the materials.

If you want to pass on my contact information, we can try to help them.

Blake Bowers, Chief
Lanton VFD
West Plains, MO
(Recipient of a 22k grant for SCBA in the first year AFG)

VP Operations
Frosty Towers Inc
www.frostytowers.com

My friends, I hope you are as happy as I am to see such a wonderful gesture of interstate mutual aid. I quickly notified Dick Doan of Posey Township of this magnificent gesture. Dick was quite happy when I spoke with him this evening. Here is his email response to me.

Hello Brothers Harry & Jack,

Harry, I appreciate the connection to Chief Bowers and will make contact with him. It would be very helpful to have the tower up and I haven't found a better price. Your idea of a story about one grant recipient helping another is wonderful.

It seems that you are beginning to make a lot of progress in getting the band back together. This time the band is the Brotherhood of Firefighters.

Dick

My friends, when you start out on a journey you never really know where things are going to wind up. My friends, this journey has taken a really neat turn. I am hoping that Chief Doan and Chief Bowers are able to work this out. Dick mentioned to me that he checked out the website for Chief Bower's company and there are a number of really big projects planned up near Posey Township.

Wow. I am hoping.

Antioch, Illinois July 19, 2006

The Home of Good Food and a Great Fire Department

T oday started off far better than I ever would have imagined. Not only did Jack and I have another fine **Hampton Inn** breakfast, but we got to enjoy a down-to-earth philosophical discussion with a really neat person. Linda Bubbe is the honcho of the Breakfast Area at the Inn, but she is far more than that my friends. She is an informed observer of the human condition.

Over a fine breakfast of eggs and sausage, she regaled Jack and me with views of the world that caused me to alternately smile and tear up. We went from the Vietnam War through the Gulf War to the current state of war in the Middle East. We shared our worries for the troops and our concerns for the future. We shared our concerns about the world our children will inherit. The coffee and the human contact were equal parts of great.

My friends, in addition to being practicing philosopher, Linda is a real hard worker, splitting her time between the Inn and another job at the Milwaukee airport. She told us that she normally works from Monday through Sunday at the Hampton Inn, but that she had to take a day off on Friday to bake three pies for an anniversary party.

I must tell you that I have met one fine American citizen in Linda Bubbe. Matt Landgraf, her hotel general manager called her, "my diamond." He went on to say that, "...she typifies all that is good and portrays what we want people to see about our hotel." I can understand that. The Milwaukee Hampton Inn was a high point on our tour.

Anyway, after awhile it was time to hit the road for today's visit in Antioch, Illinois. The ride down I-94 was spectacularly unspectacular until we almost missed the turnoff to U.S. Highway 45 just over the border from Wisconsin to Illinois. The signs in Wisconsin were numbered in the 350-mile range. Suddenly there was a welcome to Illinois sign and then suddenly, WHAM Exit 1-B Highway 45.

Wow, what an instant welcome to the region. After just a few short miles on Illinois 173, I began to feel, for some strange reason, like I was at home. I did not immediately know why, but it began to dawn on me as we continued on. The region around Antioch, Illinois was an area in flux.

There were still farm fields on both sides of the road, but there were also a great many cars all around us. Then it hit me. The Antioch area was undergoing the same metamorphosis that my home town underwent in the 1980's and 1990's. I call it the "farm to farm-less syndrome."

The Yahoo map directions took us to the geographic center of Antioch, which was really out in the middle of nowhere. So Jack and I started circling around the blocks moving toward what seemed to be the actual downtown business area. Since we were a bit early for our meeting with Lieutenant Chris Lienhardt, Jack and I did a little exploring. There were brand new houses across the street from lovely fields of corn. There were old established businesses intermingled with brand new shopping centers. I will be darned if I didn't feel a bit homesick.

Eventually we made the right turn that took us to the old downtown area of the Village of Antioch. It was indeed another lovely slice of small town America. Many of the buildings bore the name of the original businesses which built them from the late 1800's and on into the early 1900's.

As we rounded the bend on Main Street near Orchard, we spotted the fire station. We pulled into the parking lot and after catching up on a few phone calls went around to the front of the station and there we found our host, Lt. Chris Lienhardt waiting to meet us. After meeting a number of the on-duty troops, we went up to the administrative offices to meet the Fire Chief Dennis Volling.

Chief Volling leads a medium-sized volunteer/paid-on-call department. The 90 members of the department protect more than 19,400 residents within the 40 square miles of their response area. Last year they responded to more than 900 calls for assistance. In addition to their local commitments, they are part of the Mutual Aid Box Alarm System (M.A.B.A.S.).

According to Chris, they have commitments to respond to any of the 28 other communities in Lake County, the Northeastern half of McHenry County, and all of Kenosha County across the border in Wisconsin. In addition, as part of the Illinois State system they even have greater alarm commitments as far away as Chicago. I want you to know that things are pretty well organized out here. I also heard the same things about regional mutual aid up in Cudahy.

There are a number of challenges located within their response area. They protect the Metra North Commuter rail line and the Wisconsin Central rail line both of which divide their community. The rail lines have continued to grow in importance and therefore are experiencing an increase in rail traffic. Residents are now able to travel from Antioch to O'Hare Airport in Chicago. They can then transfer to local rail transport to reach downtown Chicago.

In addition, they have 35 marinas located on their portion of the Chain of Lakes region. There are 11 schools in their response area, as well as fifteen houses of worship and over 8,000 housing units.

Given their location between Chicago and Milwaukee (just about half way between the two) they are experiencing a housing boom. They have seen more than 2,100 homes and a variety of "big box" stores built in the last two years. The demand for their services has increased proportionally.

They operate a fleet of four engines, two tenders, one squad unit, one ladder truck, three brush trucks, and a fire investigation unit. They also operate a dive unit van, a boat, a rehab unit and three support vehicles. This equipment operates out of three stations located around the community.

The department also operates a fairly unique staffing setup. Every day from 0600 to 1800 hrs, members of the department are on in-station standby. They receive an hourly rate and are in the stations, available to response as needed. Each of the people to whom we spoke had high praise for the system.

While we were in town, the department boat was summoned to a water rescue operation in a mutual aid community. Sadly the operation was not successful. The department dive team was on standby, but was not called to the scene of the incident.

The department received their FIRE Act grant in 2004. It allowed them to purchase personal protection equipment, radios, and a thermal imaging camera. They also were funded for RIT fittings for their SCBA. Chris mentioned that the grant allowed them to purchase things that they could not otherwise have afforded. Once again Jack and I met a fire department wherein the morale has improved greatly with the addition of the new turnout gear and other equipment.

During our visit we also got to meet for a short time with Drew Smith of the Prospect Heights Fire Department. During our discussions he shared a sentiment with us that he wanted passed along to the fire service, as well as to the Members of Congress who need to realize the importance of the FIRE Act grant program.

"It is the catalyst for change in the fire service," he noted. "The program is bringing people together in ways not previously seen." What he said echoed the comments made at just about every one of our stops on the road trip. People are coming together in ways not previously seen. The FIRE Act is bringing the fire service together.

Chris Lienhardt was pleased to relate a very important success story to Jack and me about the thermal imaging equipment they received from the FIRE Act grant program. He stated that they responded to a reported structure fire in a downtown Main Street business establishment. When they arrived, smoke was coming out of every floor of the building and beginning to peek through the roof.

They were able to use the imaging camera to quickly locate the source of the fire in a sidewall. They opened up the walls and extinguished the fire. Chris told us that in the old days, they would have had a tough time locating the fire by the old trial-and-error method.

"That camera probably saved about four attached buildings down on Main Street," Chris noted. "These were all older, attached structures with balloon frame construction. Without the grant-funded equipment we might not have found the fire in time to extinguish the fire and save the structure.

The complex of buildings makes up about 25 percent of our downtown business district" Once again Jack and I encountered an instance where FIRE Act funds had a direct impact upon the operational efficiency and effectiveness of a grant recipient. That is what this Road Trip is all about.

I would like to make special mention of the refreshments provided for our news conference with the local papers. Kathleen Miedema's Éclair Dessert was succulent and Barbara Reulbach's Autumn Apple Bundt Cake was outstanding. The fire department was kind enough to give Jack and I each a copy of their Firehouse Favorites Cookbook: a fund-raising effort of the Antioch Firefighter's Association. Jack and I also got personal instruction on how to make these two taste treats. I for one will leave the cooking to my darling wife Jackie.

Not long after completing our final discussions with Chris, we bid a fond farewell to him and the fine folks who staff the Antioch Fire Department. Next stop: Bourbonnais, Illinois.

Bourbonnais, Illinois July 20, 2006

Home of the Community Fire Department and the One-Inch Steak

Jack and I hit the road this morning headed south from Antioch, Illinois to the Village of Bourbonnais, about 45 minutes south of Chicago. As we were heading out of the **Hampton Inn** in Gurnee, the skies were overcast, and a bit of lightning lit up the sky off to the south. But it did not seem too bad.

We had a hard time understanding why the radio stations were talking about four-hour flight delays and more than 100 cancellations at O'Hare Airport in Chicago. About 40 minutes later, Mother Nature gave us the answer to our questions. As we neared O'Hare on I-294, the spillways of heaven opened up and the skies overflowed. It was raining so hard that we could not see the traffic signs. I was starting to get that "nervous maybe we would be killed by a truck, feeling."

My friends, it was like driving through a car wash. Trucks were whipping by, lightning was flashing on all sides, and we were hoping that the road signs would once again be visible to humanity. It was tough. Luckily for us, our Antioch host, Chris Lienhardt, gave me the stay to the famous "stay-to-the-right" directions that kept us on track. Thank you Chris, your guidance carried the day.

Let me tell you my friends, the merge from I-294 to I-80 is one major league pain in the butt. However, without periodic rebuilding, I guess that our interstate highways would crumble and return to concrete dust. I am just glad we were not traveling in the other direction. Eastbound I-80, leading to I-294 was bumper-to-bumper traffic for more than five miles.

Once we made it to I-57 south, things calmed down considerably. The run to Bourbonnais went almost fairly well. Unfortunately the Yahoo map directions took a poop in Manteno. We found ourselves on a side street next to Catholic Church. It seemed to lead nowhere and it just didn't look right.

It was at this time that the innate Carter compass took over. I saw railroad tracks nearby and knew that Bourbonnais was on the main line south. So Jack and I, with the aid of the compass in the "grey ghost" worked our way over to Illinois Highway 50 south. I saw a sign for Kankakee and knew that Bourbonnais was right next to Kankakee. So on we rolled for about ten miles. And then there it was: a sign that said Bourbonnais to the right.

All I had to do was follow the signs leading the world to the Chicago Bear's summer camp, and there it was. Heck, there is even a giant water tower with the saying "Bourbonnais, Illinois, Home of the Chicago Bear's Summer Camp. Not more than two blocks past the tower site sits the modern quarters of the Bourbonnais Fire Protection District.

We met our host, Chief Ed St, Louis and his Deputy Jim Keener at about 1330 hrs. and proceeded to spend an enjoyable afternoon discussing the FIRE Act and the fire service in general. They also confirmed that I knew of Bourbonnais for something other than the FIRE Act.

They told me the story of the 1999 Amtrak train wreck which occurred in their community. They spoke of the death and destruction. They also spoke of the challenges to the fire protection community in the region. It is an event that I would not wish on anyone. But it made them all stronger. Word has it that the Metra Commuter network is going to move south from University Park and on past Bourbonnais.

Bourbonnais, Illinois is a city of 36,000 citizens who live within the 36 square mile area community. The fire chief even joked that the population is increasing monthly. Unfortunately, they are in danger of losing a bit of territory through annexation but they are working hard to maintain their response district.

Given the population growth they are experiencing, they are in the planning process for a second station, with a third one on the long range planning board. The mayor of their community is a strong supporter of the fire department and has even brokered the donation of land for the fire district to use for their new station. Even now they are scouting for land on the west side of the community for that third station.

The Bourbonnais Fire Protection District was formed in 1948 and for many years operated two stations in concert with the Village. From 1987 until 1994 the district staffed three stations. They now have a full-time chief and a full-time lieutenant with plans to test for and hire two additional full-time lieutenants. Very shortly the paid-on-call deputy chief, Jim Keener will become a full-time district employee.

The department has a staff of 37 paid-on-call personnel and 19 part-time flex-shift people. They operate a fleet of two pumpers, a pumper/tanker, a platform ladder, a brush truck, a boat, a haz-mat vehicle and a specialty rescue vehicle. They maintain a paid-on-call staff from 1800-0600 each day, except that on weekends and holidays it goes to a 24-hour shift. In this way, they are not burning out their whole staff for the normal array of smells and bells.

They maintain a 24/7 EMS unit that always has a paramedic and an EMT on duty. Sometimes they even have two paramedics on duty depending on shift scheduling. They also have an engineer on duty 24/7 and a firefighter from 0600-2200 hr. Many times extra personnel bunk in overnight. This allows them to get their rigs on the road faster.

In 2003 they received a FIRE Act grant that allowed them to refurbish and equip their training room. It is as good a training room as I have ever seen. They have an extensive array of audiovisual and textual support. They are now also able to serve as a regional training site.

Their 2004 grant allowed them to completely replace the personal protective equipment for their entire fire department. Chief St. Louis mentioned that the improved gear allowed his people to be more effective and efficient. They can work better now that they have modern, breathable gear. Their new leather boots have also made a great difference in their ability to work for extended periods.

It should be noted that Chief St. Louis is an instructor for the Illinois Fire Service Institute. In this capacity he gets to travel to all parts of the state. Along the way he has met a number of departments which were in need of help. As the new P.P.E. was phased in to his department, he passed along the older useable gear to departments in the southern part of the state who needed some help. As I have written many times on my road trip, this "pass-along effect" is an added benefit of the FIRE Act.

The fire protection district has also used departmental funding to supplement the safety which came from the new P.P.E. Every member of the department now has a reflective vest. They are used every time they respond. They are only removed for firefighting operations. They also have a new supply of highway safety cones and highway reflective signage. All EMS personnel have received four-season reflective yellow coats.

The Fire District has a tremendous relationship with Jerry Weller, their Member of Congress. He personally came to their firehouse each time they received their grant check. Letters of thanks also went to both U.S. Senators from the state. Chief St. Louis maintains frequent contact with both his federal and state legislators.

The Bourbonnais Fire Protection District is truly a community fire department. There is a slogan on the side of each piece of equipment which states that the equipment is "Owned by the Communities We Serve." They truly believe in this community-oriented approach to service. On a number of occasions, the department has responded to the homes of citizens to help them celebrate family events. They are firm believers in the Gospel of Community Service, as preached by Alan the Great.

Jack and I also were the guests at a community reception thrown in our honor by the fire protection district. We were lucky enough to get the full one-inch thick steaks from the local Krogers store. The garlic potatoes were to die for. There was also a salad and a healthy dessert of mixed fruit. These guys would give my old gang in Newark a run for their money in the kitchen.

We were also fortunate to spend time with Lisa Dugan, the local representative from the state legislature. We also met members from a number of surrounding departments. We met with Chief Dave Horn from Momence and his assistant Tom Turrell. There was also Assistant Chief Jerry Dole from Manteno, Chief Al Ramsey from the Herscher Fire Department, and Assistant Chief Bob Bowen from the Aroma Fire Protection District.

We had a great discussion on the role of politics and the fire service. I was greatly impressed by the knowledge that Lisa Dugan had with regard to the fire service. But I would expect that from her, because she is an active member of the Illinois Fire Caucus. I explained the purpose of my road trip and the need for her to keep interacting with Members of Congress and the U.S. Senate.

My friends, we need more legislators like Lisa Dugan. I would also like to single out F/F Greg St. Louis for special mention. After the wireless Internet at the **Hampton Inn** took a poop, he was able to get me up and running on the Bourbonnais Fire Protection District's WI-FI network. We need more computer-literate people like him in the fire service.

In the morning I will follow the rail track south as Jack and I jump on I-57 and head for Tennessee.

Gilt Edge, Tennessee July 21, 2006

A Taste of Southern Hospitality

My friends, I actually broke a woman's heart this morning. As I was checking out of the Hampton Inn the kindly front desk person was printing out our bill when she said, "Dr. Carter, you are the one who is taking the road trip about fire departments, aren't you?" When I responded that I was, she told me that she had heard about our trip and about our continuing mention of the **Hampton Inn** chain.

It was at this point that I told her that I had been forced to put up a bad review of her hotel. I could see the color drain out of her face. She then asked me why. I simply told the truth about my need to get on the Internet for my daily post and how the front desk clerk did not have a clue as to what to do or how to help me. I then told her how I had to keep the gang at the Bourbonnais fire house up late while I did my work.

She was apologetic. However, I could see that I had not started her day off on a high note. I thanked her for the fine breakfast, went over the buffet area, and poured a cup of the Robust blend for our trip south. I felt bad for her, but sometimes the truth leads you in that type of direction.

Today was our first really long travel leg. Our Yahoo map directions were simple and to the point. Go two blocks, make a right on Interstate Highway 57 and go 329 miles. So that is what Jack and I did. We made pretty good time, because I-57 in Illinois is a well-maintained high-speed road.

We stopped twice on the way south. Once in Illinois, for coffee and the usual highway amenities and another time just over the Missouri border. I am glad we waited to take on fuel. The price dropped from $3.12 at Antioch to $2.73 in Charlton, Missouri.

It was at this point that my brain over-rode the Yahoo map directions. Yesterday the directions were wrong, however today my brain suffered a senior moment of the first magnitude. Somehow I got it in my mind that we were going to go south to Memphis and then north to Gilt Edge. WRONG! Mickey-the-Boob that I am I failed to notice the cut off at I-155 just north of the Arkansas border.

So there we were, steaming down I-55 in eastern Arkansas. I guess I sort of got hung up on in a fog of nostalgia, as we went driving past my last base in the U.S. Air Force which was located in Blytheville, Arkansas, just over the border from Missouri. I recognized the old truck stop where I frequently ate when I was stationed there in 1970. Sadly it is now closed, replaced by the usual array of fast-food restaurants.

Just south of Blytheville I asked Jack for our trip book. A quick look at the directions told me that I had made a mistake of the first rank. Luckily I found it out in time to correct the error. I guess we added about 40 miles to the trip. But that is much better than the 120 miles it would have added had we gone down to Memphis and then back up to Gilt Edge. Later in the afternoon, after an eight-hour road rally, we rolled into Covington, Tennessee and checked into our motel on the Jefferson Davis Highway.

After checking yet another series of emails we made contact with our host Chief Steve Fletcher of the Gilt Edge, Tennessee Fire Department. His directions were as precise as any I have ever seen. I made the turn from the Jefferson Davis Highway on to Tennessee Highway 59 and proceeded 10.3 miles as directed. I then crossed a bridge and found the Gilt Edge Volunteer Fire Department located on a prominent triangle at the entrance to their small rural community.

The temperature upon our arrival was a swinging 98 degrees. The humidity was somewhere in the region of 120 to 130 percent. By golly, you would never know that we were less than six miles from the mighty Mississippi River. My warm-weather memories of Memphis, Tennessee in 1970 came racing back. After we exchanged pleasantries on the apron, the chief quickly ushered us into their air conditioned meeting/radio room.

Chief Fletcher then introduced us to Mayor Wayne Sloan and Councilman Bill Fleming. The chief wanted us to know that his department had the full support and backing of their local government. The chief also introduced us to Margaret Black, a field representative for Congressman John Tanner, their local Member of Congress. Let me tell you, we had an excellent discussion with everyone in the room chiming in with their personal views.

Gilt Edge is community of about 489 citizens in the 35 square-mile community in Tipton County. They also provide fire protection for the Town of Burleson, population 453, and about 2,550 citizens in unincorporated Tipton County. Their location near the Shelby County/Memphis region has caused a bit of a building boom in the area. Tipton is the second-fastest growing county in West Tennessee. They are the next county out from Shelby County.

There is very little industry in their fire district. The largest portion of their local industry would be farming, but only a small percentage of the population is engaged in farming. They have a number of small commercial occupancies, a repair garage, a café, a construction company, two trucking companies, and 16 churches. The majority of the population commutes to work in Shelby County, with the average trip to work being in the 30-50 mile range.

This 24-member department operates out of a single station. They have a fleet which includes a pumper, and two tankers. They also operate a small squad truck which runs on EMS and grass fire calls. They receive funding from the Town of Gilt Edge, Tipton County, and the Town of Burlison. Funding also comes from a mail-based fund-raising campaign. Chief Fletcher mentioned that the returns from the fund drive are down a bit this year, but he attributes that to the increased cost of gasoline, as well as utility prices.

They received FIRE Act grants in 2002, 2003, 2004, and 2005. In 2002 they received personal PASS devices, and a new accountability system. They also received new gloves and goggles. In 2003 they received grant funding to install an automatic fire sprinkler system in their station. They also received two automatic emergency defibrillators (AED), training for CPR instructors and CPR training aids. In addition, they also received new portable radios.

Their 2004 grant provided a new commercial pumper and the necessary hose and equipment. They donated their old 1971 pumper to a small nearby department who went on to lose both of their 1960-vintage pumpers to mechanical problems. As a matter of fact, their old pumper came from the South Old Bridge Fire Department which is located near where I live in New Jersey.

In 2005 their grant allowed them to acquire new SCBA units, a cascade system with a fill station, another AED, a thermal imagining camera, a laptop computer, and an LCD projector. They were also able to have a Fire Instructor I class delivered in their station which qualified a dozen members as state-certified fire instructors.

Chief Fletcher told Jack and I that the grants have made a difference in the future direction of their department. "The grants allowed us to move into the 21st Century," the chief proudly noted. "It would have been impossible for us to have achieved these projects on our own."

He also told us that membership is now up from what it once was. "We went from about 14 members to our current level of 23," he noted. "It is like we are a new fire department now."

The chief also invited a neighboring department to meet with Jack and me. Chief Jon Piercey of the Three Star Volunteer Fire Department spoke of the grants that his department received in 2002, 2003, and 2004. Their department also protects a small rural community in Tipton County.

Their 2002 grant allowed them to acquire new SCBA, new turnout gear, rescue extrication tools, as well as a variety of small equipment. In 2003 they were able to acquire 9000 feet of a variety of sizes of fire house, a complete radio network, including mobile, hand-held units, a base station, and repeaters. The also were able to acquire new pagers and a complete hose washing system. Their 2004 grant allowed them to acquire a new four-wheel drive combination quick attack/squad unit.

Chief Piercey told us that the impact of the FIRE Act grants was like something akin to the starting of a new fire department. "It would have taken us several years to complete just one of these purchases," he mentioned. "The new vehicle has allowed us to improve our response to highway incidents in our area."

Chief Piercey told us that a lot of their old gear and equipment consisted of hand-me-downs from the Memphis Fire Department. He mentioned that they were able to donate a lot of their hose to other departments in the area when their grant-supplied hose arrived. However, he said that most of their old turnout gear and

SCBA units were too outdated to donate to other departments.

Chief Fletcher and Chief Piercey stressed that they thought it was essential to keep the peer review process for the grants. "That process is so great that the whole federal government should think about using it for all of their grant programs," Chief Fletcher stressed.

Both chiefs also urged Ms. Black to take their concerns about fully funding the FIRE Act to the billion dollar level to Congressman Tanner. I supported their efforts by sharing many of the success stories I have seen on the road trip. She indicated that the Congressman is a strong support of the FIRE Act. I thanked her for the support.

My friends, I saw two fire departments who were allowed to enter the 21st Century thanks to the vision of Congressman Bill Pascrell and the folks who helped to create this landmark legislation. Jack and I were also treated to an ample helping of "Southern Hospitality" after the meeting was concluded. I do not know how we are doing it, but our clothes still seem to fit. I guess I will really know next week when I have to don my sport coat in Baltimore for the Firehouse Expo.

Well my friends, B and B will try to get a good night's rest to prepare us for tomorrows run to Smithville, Tennessee.

Smithville, Tennessee July 22, 2003

I Have Seen Small Town America
at its Finest

Let me begin this day's blog entry with an apology to every hotel or motel where I stayed prior to last night and whose praises I did not sing. I am sorry my friends, I guess I have just been spoiled by the good fortune of my life. I called the Bates chain and had them take their Champaign, Illinois unit off of the do not call list.

Thankfully this was my last night in a non-major brand facility. It will be greater than 85 percent **Hampton Inns** for the rest of the trip. Yes my friends, Harry has owned up to being a spoiled hotel visitor. During the night, Jack and I counted at least ten trains as they noisily tooted their way through downtown Covington, Tennessee.

If you have any doubts about the strength and activity of the rail industry in America, let me put your fears to rest. My trip through the heart of our country has reinforced my faith in and love of the railroads of our nation. I just wish our government would wake up to this fact. I may still make that great cross-country train journey which I have dreamed about some time now. Who knows, that may be how I visit the fire service out west.

Since our hotel did not offer any form of a complimentary breakfast, we hit the road a little earlier than planned. Thanks again to Steve Fletcher. He gave me another one of his fine sets of local directions with a precise series of left, right, and left on the road to Brownsville style turns. He probably shaved about 20 miles off of our trip to Smithville. After yesterday's series of wrong turns, that is a good thing.

Today's trip across Tennessee went quite well. The directions given to me by Chief Donny Green from the De Kalb County Fire Department were right on target. Luckily for us the Smithville, Tennessee area is right on U.S. 70. Once we hit the downtown area of the city, Donny was able to guide us to their headquarters station about four miles out of the city in the De Kalb County area.

The county is irregularly shaped thanks to the Center Hill Dam which was built during 1942-1943. It is one of the power production dams which form the Tennessee Valley Authority. The dam created a major lake which has become a choice recreational area. However, it has made for some very long runs for the fire department. There are nine marinas located around the lake which create a special marine firefighting hazard for the department.

The Center Lake area has become a choice spot for the building of modern lakefront homes. Chief Green noted that now, "people want that big, beautiful home on the lakefront."

The De Kalb County Fire Department is an all-volunteer agency which was founded in 1975. They protect their area from a series of ten stations located throughout the 305-square mile county area. None of the stations is what I might call sumptuous. They are all small, simple metal clad structures.

In their early years, the department had to battle for every cent of aid that they could. Over the years the department has become involved in the local political process. They had to become active in order to elect people who are supportive or the fire department. Currently, Assistant Chief Roy Merriman is a county commissioner.

"Our county now has the desire to help us," Chief Green noted. "It has been a battle, but we have won over a lot of people who were originally against the department." According to several members with whom I spoke, the County Mayor, Mike Foster, has been an ardent supporter of the fire department.

Chief Green told us that when he became the chief in 1994, the total budget for the department was less than $14,000. Over the years they have managed to push that number up to its current level of just over $110,000. That seems like a lot, but when you spread it over the ten (soon to be eleven) stations, it seems to fall a bit short of meeting all of their needs.

In their apparatus fleet, they have only five rated pumper units. With the exception of the new unit acquired with the 2003 FIRE Act grant, their other units are all 1970's vintage apparatus. That would include their four Class A pumpers, and the rest of the fleet which all are smaller, home-made units with Wisconsin gas engines installed to run the pumps which are mounted on the back.

These units pump the water out of the tanks which were crafted onto the original chassis's which the county acquired in 1975. They can only supply up to 250 gallons though. All of the original unrated pumpers were built locally by a vocational education class. In my area we would think of these as super-sized brush units, but here in De Kalb County they serve as frontline fire attack units.

In the early years of the department, before they ever had any structures, the equipment was parked along side of local businesses. If there was a call the police dispatchers would notify the business owner who would round up whoever he could find. During the winter, they had to drain the tanks so that if a fire came in they had to respond to a place where they could fill the unit up with water before responding to the incident.

At this time, the department is on the verge of opening a new station. The nine new members for that station are in the process of completing the 64-hour state training program. The department is not sure exactly how they will provide the turnout gear for these folks. I would guess that there will be a lot of searching in the supply locker for gear that will fit the troops.

There are currently 63 members serving the county. The department responds to over 1,000 fire and EMS calls each year. The department is fortunate in that a number of local companies allow their people to leave work to respond to calls for assistance during the daytime period.

Even with this, many of their daytime runs are handled by a minimum number of people. It is not unusual to have one or two people performing the initial operations at incidents. A number of the members told me that they have to make do with whoever shows up on any given day.

In 2001 they received 40 full sets of turnout gear from their FIRE Act grant. They also received 20 self-contained breathing apparatus (SCBA) units and 30 spare cylinders. In addition to this they acquired 40 PASS devices. In 2003 the FIRE Act grant allowed them to purchase their first (and only) brand-new piece of frontline firefighting apparatus. It is the "Queen of the Fleet."

In 2004 they received a grant to create a fire prevention effort. They were able to get 1,000 smoke detectors, 2,000 nine-volt batteries, a laptop computer, an LCD projector, and a series of fire prevention videos and classroom supplies. Since then they have conducted an extensive smoke detector training program. Many of the members went out to install smoke detectors in homes throughout the county on their own time.

They now conduct fire training programs in all of the county's schools. They have visited every third, fourth, and fifth grade class in each of the elementary schools. They have taught other programs in each of the other schools. They also conduct senior citizen's fire training at the senior centers throughout the county.

The department is extremely proud of the fact that they have recorded two actual saves in homes that received fire department-installed smoke detectors. In both cases the families were able to evacuate without any injuries. In one case, the department was notified in time to response and save the home. These are two more critical saves that can be chalked up in the plus column for the FIRE Act.

Chief Green also spoke of their extensive training program. He told us of the many hours devoted each year to honing their skills and learning new ones. They now have a nice central classroom area in their new fire headquarters. The building formerly served as a Tennessee Highway Department road garage. With the help of their county government and state legislators, they were able to acquire the building and convert it into their headquarters station.

"We now have a central focus around which to rally our department," Chief Green proudly noted. "We can now come together and train as a department.

It should also be mentioned that there is no water system in the county. This has forced the entire department to become experts in the use and identifying of alternative water sources. Jack and I gave them a few hints on how to stretch their resources.

We got to see one of the largest tree nurseries in the world. De Kalb County is the second largest nursery county in the world, second only to neighboring Warren County. The trees seemed to go on forever as we looked across the wide expanse of fertile, sloping fields. While visiting this facility Jack showed the chief a couple of pumping points where a fire department connection could be installed and made a part of the operation. The chief told us that he would pursue that one in the coming weeks.

The highlight of the day for Jack and I was the chance that we had to see a real slice of small town America. The fire department was holding its annual fish fry at their Belk Station, which was located about 15 miles outside of the downtown Smithville area. Jack and I were invited to partake in the festivities.

The event at the county community center next to the fire station was filled to capacity with local citizens who came out to support the department and enjoy some of the best fish I have ever had. This was small town America at its finest. We got to enjoy an outstanding meal and meet a number of the local candidates for political office who were on the stump for support.

Since the election is just ten days away, the campaign was rolling along in high gear. There was a great deal of friendly bantering as each candidate stood up to make their pitch for support. I was surprised and honored when the Station Commander, Lieutenant James Pennington introduced Jack and me and asked for me to say a few words.

My friends, I now have no doubt about the wide ranging impact of Firehouse Magazine and Firehouse.com. I had one firefighter tell me about the monthly battle over who is going to read the magazine first in their home. Here I was, in a small town in Middle Tennessee hearing the praises of our magazine sung by person after person.

As we were about to leave Chief Green told me, "We are so many years ahead of where we would be if it wasn't for the FIRE Act." He urged Jack and me to tell the story of the impact of this important legislation in his community. He thanked us for our efforts, and wished us well in our battle to raise the FIRE Act to its full authorized level of a billion dollars.

I felt absolutely great as we rode west into the setting sun toward the Hampton Inn in Murfreesboro. Jack and I had a great day in De Kalb County, Tennessee. Tomorrow we are heading on south to Clanton, Alabama.

East Chilton, Alabama July 23, 2006

I Witnessed an Act of Christian Kindness Today

The conclusion of our visit with East Clanton, Alabama was really special. I saw an act of Christian charity on the part of the members of a small rural volunteer fire department. However, I will leave that for the end of this blog visit.

Today was a fairly routine day on the road. Of course if you consider traveling through three states over a 10-hour day and, 420 miles routine then you have either been on the on the road too long or you are a professional truck driver and are just warming up. Traffic headed south on I-24 out of Murfreesboro, Tennessee was pretty tough until it started to break up about 50 miles into our journey.

Our daily routine now involves contacting our host early in the day to assure them that we are on the road and headed their way. Jack and I have also learned to mention our directions, just in case there is a better way of traveling to the host's community.

Good that we did this, because our host, Deputy Chief Dan Wright of the East Chilton Volunteer Fire Department cut about 15 miles off our journey.

When we arrived in East Chilton, we were greeted by the sight of their gleaming white equipment lined up in parade ground order outside of their small, rural station. We pulled into the lot and began shaking hands all around. The department had turned out the majority of their staff for our get-together. Deputy Chief Wright then introduced me to their Chief, Matt Griffin.

Let me tell you something my friends. This department has to be one of the youngest groups of firefighters that I have met in a long time. There are about 20 members who belong to this department which was founded in 1977.

The East Chilton Volunteer Fire Department protects a 32-square mile unincorporated area of Chilton County just outside of the city limits of Clanton. The estimates of their population range from 3,800 to 4,000. Chief Wright told us that it is hard to get a handle on just how many people are in the community because there is no dedicated census tract for an unincorporated area. They fall under the Clanton census tract, so their population has to be estimated.

There is not much industry to speak of outside of a small family-owned cabinet shop, a storage warehouse and a trucking company in their area. Most of the community consists of residential and farming areas. There is also a great deal of timberland within their response district. They are concerned that any attempts at developing commercial enterprises will be annexed into Clanton.

They have a good working relationship with the neighboring department in Clanton. Many times during the year the department responds into the city to assist their volunteer department. They are on mutual aid assignment to a number of industrial occupancies in Clanton.

The department has gone from responding to less than 100 calls a few years ago to a level of more than 200 calls last year. Runs in the department are up this year. They are on par to move above the 200 level again this year.

Funding for the department comes from a county mill tax. The funds are received by the county tax collector and distributed equally to all rural fire departments in the county. Unfortunately, as areas of the country become prosperous they are annexed, and the money for those areas is lost to all of the county fire departments. This seems odd to me, however it is the way that a great many states in the union operate. This makes growth a sort of two-edged sword.

The department received one FIRE Act grant in 2004. They received 12 new self-contained breathing apparatus (SCBA) units, as well as 12 spare cylinders. In addition they received ten complete sets of turnout gear, a rapid intervention kit and a host of training materials. In addition they received a complete set of extrication equipment, which includes cutters, spreaders, ram, and a power unit capable of operating two units at once. They also received a thermal imaging camera and a set of airbags.

Chief Griffin told us that they are now able to deliver a new service to their community thanks to the FIRE Act grant program. "We can now do rescue and extrication work for our citizens," Chief Griffin noted. "Before we had to respond to accidents, assess the situation and call help from Clanton. Now we can get started right away with our own tools."

The department is also experiencing an increased number of calls for their new equipment. "People are now calling us for our thermal imaging camera and extrication equipment," Chief Wright mentioned. "Things are getting busier in our area and sometimes Clanton is tied up and we need to help."

Many of the members present spoke to the fact that there is a great deal more training going on. "In the old days, when we only had the six SCBA, it was hard to train with them, because we had to take turns sharing the air capacity." Chief Griffin told us. "We now have enough of a capacity to get everyone on air. It is much better now."

The members all mentioned that the new P.P.E. gave them an added sense of confidence during their drills and during their firefighting operations. "Last year we were lucky enough to get five houses to burn for training," Chief Griffin said. "Normally we are lucky to get one. This allowed us to do a great deal more with our new gear and SCBA."

To date the department has received one grant. They have applied four times. They have hopes that they will get another one at some time in the future. The department also has a great aid in Chief Wright's wife Wendy. It just seems that she is the assistant EMA director for Chilton County.

During our discussions, she mentioned the success that her office has had in generating other funding for the county. She herself has attended the Emergency Management Institute in Emmitsburg and was able to relate some neat Ott House stories. Last time around she was the student and her husband the chief went along for the ride. By all accounts they had a pretty good time.

Each person to whom I spoke applauded the Chilton County communication's system. They mentioned that it is a great help and allows everyone to communicate during emergencies. Like I have said many times in the past, a good communications system lies at the heart of every efficient operation we have ever seen. Chilton County is no different.

After a simply scrumptious supper of good, Southern pork barbeque and home-made cakes, Jack and I were preparing to depart for our evening's rest stop when we saw an act of Christian charity take place in front of our very eyes.

Jack and I were one our way out to the "grey ghost" to load

up, when we saw the entire body of East Clanton firefighters gathered around their chief and a Chief from a neighboring county who had stopped by for my visit. I could not make out the group's discussions, but I heard someone yell out, "...all in favor aye." There was a group cheer of Aye and many raised their hands in support of the motion, whatever it was.

I edged closer to see what was going on. It turned out that Chief Brannon Walter of the Weogufka Volunteer Fire Department was relating a tale of woe about a fire department in his area that had just lost their aging fire truck to an electrical fire. He was asking the assembled throng to donate the old East Chilton pumper, which was sitting out behind their station, to that department.

Deputy Chief Wright explained to me that they had quickly called a special meeting of the department and voted to give the distressed department their old vehicle. Chief Griffin also mentioned that this was the department to whom they donated their old SCBA which had been replaced by the FIRE Act equipment.

By golly, that was a great thing to observe. As a matter of fact Chief Walter drove over from his station in another county to show us the pumper that his department received from the FIRE Act. I am creating a special post for the meeting of many departments that took place after my visit with East Clanton.

Jack and I saw the real fire service at work today. These are people who are taking time out of their lives to help their neighbors. Now they are better able to do their work thanks to the FIRE Act.

East Chilton, Alabama July 23, 2006

Part II - Another Meeting of the Minds

The story continues for my visit to East Chilton, Alabama. After my extensive interviews with Chief Matt Griffin and Deputy Chief Dan Wright of the East Chilton Volunteer Fire Department, a series of guests began arriving at their fire station. They had all traveled a far piece to meet with me. Each had journeyed from one to three hours to meet with me in order to share their stories.

Assistant Chief Jeff Monroe of the Five Points Volunteer Fire Department had emailed me asking if he and some other fire officers could meet with me at East Chilton. I advised him to make contact with Dan Wright and we would go from there. This was a fortunate thing, because it allowed me to meet a number of other FIRE grant recipients who wished to share their success stories with me. They were:

- Chief Monroe from the Five Points Fire Department
- Captain Mark Allred from the Kellyton Volunteer Fire Department
- Assistant Chief Buster Bolton from the Winterboro Volunteer Fire/Rescue
- Chief Brannon Walter from the Weogufka Volunteer Fire Department
- Chief Greg Mask from the County Line Volunteer Fire Department

This was a special meeting of the minds, for you see, each of these departments has received a new piece of fire apparatus from the FIRE Act program. I have to stress that each of these gentlemen comes from different counties. These gentlemen have also formed an informal network to share their thoughts on how to work with the FIRE Act program and a number of other continuing issues.

These departments protect areas that range in size from 40-90 square miles and populations which range from about 800 to slightly over 3,000 people. Their budgets are all small and much of their firefighting apparatus fleets is older. One chief even mentioned that there had never been a new fire truck in his county until the FIRE Act provided one to his department.

Each officer in attendance spoke of their strong support for the existing FIRE Act peer-review system. These gentlemen also mentioned that they had been working hard to convince their Members of Congress of the need to fully fund the program in order to help more departments.

Jeff Monroe related the fact that in those instances where new apparatus was received by the five departments that each received a personal phone call from Representative Mike Rogers. He also spoke of a regional seminar conducted by Congressman Spenser Bachus. The seminar was designed to teach the attendees how to apply for a number of different grant programs, among them the FIRE Act.

These five chief fire officers spoke of how they were, "burning up the phone wires" to convince their Congressman of the need to fully fund the act. Chief Monroe also mentioned that they are working on an effort to get their Congressmen to push for the reauthorization of the FIRE Act which is due to happen next year.

In reviewing the pictures of the apparatus which were replaced by the new FIRE Act acquisitions, Jack and I saw some pretty old equipment. Their ages ranged from the early 1960's through the early 1980's. Each of these gentlemen expressed their appreciation for the changes which their FIRE Act grants allowed them to experience.

Apparatus was not the only thing received by a couple of the departments. In addition to the new pumper which Kellyton received from the 2004 Fire Act grant, they were able to get new SCBA and turnout gear in 2005. Five Points received P.P.E., and SCBA in 2003, the new vehicle in 2004, and EMS gear, a thermal imaging camera, and rescue tools in 2005. They also received a Fire Prevention grant in 2005 which allowed them to create a Learn-Not-To-Burn program for their schools and acquire 911 address signs for the community.

After I met with these folks we all took advantage of the East Chilton Fire Company's hospitality. I expressed my gratitude to these fine men for taking their time to travel a great distance to meet with Jack and me. After taking our leave, Jack and I continued on to Auburn, Alabama in order to enjoy another night with the **Hampton Inn** folks.

Tomorrow it is off to Albemarle, North Carolina. We are looking at about eight hours on the road. I guess you might say it is just a piece of cake, as it were.

Albemarle, North Carolina July 24, 2006

The Home of Hospitality and Fine Haircuts

My friends, I am glad to be alive. No, this is not the beginning of some philosophical study on life. I am just glad to be alive. There was a moment this morning on the outskirts of Atlanta, Georgia when this condition was in doubt. As Jack and I were merging onto I-85 from the by-pass I-285 our lives were almost cut short by a young Georgia Peach.

There was a giant sign which read **LANE ENDS AHEAD**. I saw this sign and was in the lane which did NOT end ahead. All of a sudden there was a small white car in my lane trying to grab the same space that the "Grey Ghost" was using quite well. My choices were to hit her, hit a Jersey barrier to the right, or jam on the brakes and pray.

I chose number three. God bless the anti-lock braking system installed by my new friends at a GM plant in Texas. My car slowed quickly, stayed under control, and did not hit the Georgia Peach, or the Jersey barrier. I was so shocked by this whole event that neither a profane word left my lips nor an obscene gesture came to mind. I guess I am a disgrace to the folks in New Jersey.

Chief Eddie McDaniel was a most genial host. We spent a great deal of time discussing his fire department and traveling through his community. He is a most accommodating man. He is also a born problem-solver. While we were chatting at their Fire Station #One, I mentioned to him that Jack and I were on the lookout for a barber. After two and a half weeks on the road, we were both beginning to look a little rough around the edges.

He saw to it that we were transported to the Modern Barbershop in downtown Albemarle. It was there that Greg gave each of us a real nice haircut and some good, old-fashioned barbershop chit chat. We talked about football, as well as the differences between my New York Giants and his Carolina Panthers. He owned up to the fact that he had never been to New Jersey. However, as he was cutting Jack's hair he admitted to having relatives from Massachusetts.

My trip to Albemarle, North Carolina today involved the longest run, in miles, of any for the whole trip. We traveled just over 500 miles to meet with my buddy Shawn Oke of the Albemarle Fire Department. I have long looked forward to meeting a man that I have mentored from afar for many years now.

Of course there was just one small problem. My host was not in town. After inviting me to visit Albemarle, he left town to attend a class at the National Fire Academy. Some host: a born-flat leaver. I even offered to call Denis at the National Fire Academy and ask him to send Shawn home for the day.

It should be noted that Shawn sent his father Bill Oke to represent him at my fire station visit. Bill is a retired member of the Fairfax, Virginia Fire Department and now serves as a fire consultant. Well, now there's my kind of a guy. We bonded well, as most consultants do. He was a good replacement.

Albemarle is a community that grew to prominence during the days when textile plants were cranking out materials for our nation's clothing industry. The plants are gone having been replaced by light industry, commercial development, and retail stores. The fire department has traced its origins to the late 19th century, but cannot be sure of the exact date.

Currently there are 16,000 residents living within the 16-square miles of the city limits. The department operates a fleet of two Quints and one Class A pumper in frontline service and one Class A pumper in reserve. There are thirty nine members in the suppression force, a fire marshal, an administrative assistant and the fire chief in this all career force.

In addition to the regular array of hazards, they provide support to the North Carolina Air National Guard at the local general aviation airport. Although there are no commercial flights at this time, plans are underway to extend the current runway by about a mile. I see growth in the offing for this area.

Work is underway to dualize the NC 24/47 route to Albemarle from Charlotte. Chief Daniels feels that this dualization project will open up the area to commuters seeking to live in a rural environment. Jack and I shared some stories about how our hometowns had been overrun with new homes by developers keen to make a buck without helping the communities where the homes were being built.

Albemarle's 2002 FIRE Act grant allowed them to develop a fire prevention program. They were able to acquire a number of laptop computers, various educational materials and a radio controlled robot "Sparky the Fire Dog". They already had a fire safety house which had been built by a local vocational education group. These folks assisted the department in building the trailer. Part of the grant also went towards a tow vehicle for the house. This vehicle is also used by the fire marshal.

In 2004 they were able to acquire 40 new self-contained

breathing apparatus units and 40 spare cylinders. The department also acquired regulators for each member. In addition to the SCBA, they acquired a compressed air fill system with a cascade unit built into it. They also received a test bench to test the regulators.

14 portable radios were also part of the mix. "We now have one portable radio for each member on duty," Chief McDaniel said. "Our old radios were held together by tape. In addition, many of our SCBA units were at or beyond their expiration dates. I had to rent cylinders to keep some of our SCBA units in service. We are much safer now."

I was also most fortunate to meet with Chris Allan, the fire chief in neighboring New London. They are an all-volunteer unit located near Albemarle. His department received FIRE Act grants in 2003 and 2004. Thanks to a two-year effort, they were able to equip, train, and field the only RIT-capable fire department in their county.

The grant funds enabled them to acquire eight new SCBA units and upgrade eight existing units for a total of 16. They also acquired 16 new cylinders and eight handheld radios. They concentrated on multiples for eight in order to provide an initial RIT team of four members and a backup team of four. In addition they have acquired a thermal imaging camera and a RIT bag for use by the team.

"The new equipment and training has sparked a new enthusiasm among our members," Chief Allan noted. "The new equipment spurred a new interest in training. We are now a safer and more capable department."

In addition to the two fire chiefs, I got to speak with Eric Wilson, a constituent liaison from the Concord office of Congressman Robin Hayes, their 8th District Representative. I explained the purpose of my road trip and offered a number of success stories to outline the impact of the FIRE Act. I thanked him for coming and urged him to share our message with the Congressman.

In addition, I met with a reporter from the local newspaper and a kindly young lady from the local television station. My friends, I guess the grind of the journey is starting to get to me. I forgot to get her name. She was a kind and gracious interviewer.

Once again I shared my Road Trip message. I urged her to get the word out that this grant program has the potential to impact every citizen in the country, if only we can get the Congress and Senate to recognize our true value and get behind our efforts.

I had been warned to arrive in Albemarle with a good appetite. For weeks now I had been hearing Shawn Oke sing the praises of the chefs in his fire department. My friends, his praises fell short of the excellence of the supper prepared for me and Jack by the gang at Station One.

It has been ages since I have had baked chicken with Pinto beans, cabbage (mild and hot) corn bread (with and without jalapeño peppers, fried squash fritters, and garlic potatoes; all washed down with several pitchers of sweet ice tea. This bill of fare was followed by about ten kinds of pies, cakes, and other desserts.

Jack and I are afraid that we will not be able to eat again until Wednesday. What makes all of this even more special is that Chief McDaniel brought the entire shift together for a communal meal in our honor. We broke bread and then we busted horns. This was a classic fire house feast.

While I was meeting with the media and the Congressional aide, Jack was out by the Quint holding court on his favorite topic: pump operations. He had the youngster's heads spinning with his ability to offer ten ways to make the pumps sing. Perhaps Chief McDaniel got a bit more than he bargained for when he invited us to his city. There is now a new generation of Jack Peltier clones in Albemarle. God help Shawn Oke when he gets back from the National Fire Academy.

It was really hard to tear ourselves away. As we were getting ready to leave, Chief McDaniel brought the entire shift together and presented us with a number of fine gifts. We received fire department tee shirts and patches. Then one of the members stepped forward and presented me with a gigantic bakery box filled to the brim with goodies from their favorite local bakery. We now have enough baked goods to get us to California and back.

A great time was had by all in Albemarle. Now it's on to Wilson, North Carolina tomorrow for a meeting with my buddy Don Oliver.

Wilson, North Carolina July 25, 2006

Home of Technology, Teaching, and My First Birthday Party of the Trip

Today was a great day. Jack and I got to catch up on same back sleep. That was a real blessing. As you might imagine, the impact of 19 days on the road does have a cumulative effect. But we are better now. Our trip from Albemarle, North Carolina to Wilson, North Carolina was actually a breeze. We have seen some really beautiful state highways during our journey. North Carolina 24/27 is among the best.

Today was oil change day. After 18 days and 4,500 miles, it was time to take the "Grey Ghost" in for some service. Let me tell you, Jim and the gang at the Jiffy Lube are a really polite and efficient group. They had me in and out in 25 minutes.

While I was at the Jiffy Lube, I got a call from my host and good buddy, Fire Chief Don Oliver. He asked if I was really coming or was the whole visit a put up job. I assured him that I was in town and enjoying the services of the local Jiffy Lube. He said to be sure to say hi to Jim for him. This I did.

Wilson Fire/Rescue Services protects close to 50,000 people living in an area of 23.2 square miles. Founded in 1881, they operate out of 5 stations which protect a primarily residential area. Their department is a public agency whose members are all career personnel. Wilson is a growth area. It is estimated that the population is growing about two percent a year. Jack and I saw a great deal of commercial development. This is a good clue that people are coming.

The department offers state of the art service (and I am not kidding on this one) and continues to pioneer new ways to serve the community. Their services include: first responder emergency medical service provided by the closest fire company, technical level hazardous materials response team, pro-active fire prevention inspection programs, and innovative public education programs. These services are provided to residential, commercial, industrial, and municipal airport occupancies.

It is a good thing that Jack and I arrived rested and ready today. Don Oliver took us on whirlwind tour of the city. We visited their Fire Training Center and met the recruit class being taught at their facility. They have managed to create a nice training center with a lot of sweat and dedication. While we were there we met the folks that were building a new training maze in the back of a trailer. It looks like it will be a good addition to their facility.

Speaking of sweat, I got to meet the fire prevention staff at a joint project that the fire department is working on with the local boys and girls clubs. The fire prevention bureau was installing a residential sprinkler system in a home being rehabilitated for future occupancy. It was about 85 degrees and the humidity was hovering around 90 percent. These guys were all dirty and soaked with sweat.

They had just laid the piping in the attic and were winding up their days work. They told me that this was not a one-shot deal.

They have an ongoing relationship with Habitat for Humanity. The fire prevention gang supplies the labor and expertise to install residential sprinklers in all new Habitat Housing. I will be writing a more complete article on this program for Firehouse magazine when I get home.

Don Oliver's department has done wonderful things with their FIRE Act grant funding. Their initial grant in 2002 went to acquire self-contained breathing apparatus and hand-held portable radios. They acquired additional SCBA face-pieces so that every person can have their own. They also acquired 32 mobile radios and 24 base station units.

Their 2003 grant was used to develop a virtual reality program for training fire inspectors. Talk about bang for the buck, their program is in use in more than 400 fire departments in 47 states. Working in concert with the **Center for Public Excellence** and **Reality Response** the Wilson Fire/Rescue Service created this ground-breaking educational effort.

In 2004 their grant went for a department-wide video-conferencing system. Every station is equipped with a two-way video conferencing capability which allows the department to deliver training to every station at the same time. This grant allowed them to purchase the all the necessary cameras, monitors, and electronic equipment.

"We can now train all of our personnel at the same time to the same standard," Chief Oliver noted, "It is much more effective and efficient. We are using less fuel and subjecting the equipment to less wear and tear. Most of all our citizens do no lose the services of their local district fire company. We are providing a better level of protection for our citizens."

This program has paid great dividends for Wilson. All promotions to the rank of Engineer and above require each individual to be a certified Fire Inspector and a certified Fire Instructor. All training is accomplished in house. They are now reaching out to the community college in an effort to offer credit courses over the department network.

Deputy Chief Randy Bowman sold us that, "we believe that we are only beginning to scratch the surface of what we can do with our system. One positive benefit comes from the fact that our training people do not have to spend time teaching the same course many times. Our station officers can now devote more time to conducting surveys and performing other department duties."

Chief Oliver also mentioned that the department is reaching out to teach courses across the region. Their relationship with the Wilson Technical and Community College has provided great dividends. The video-conferencing capability provided by the FIRE Act funding is now having an impact on communities all across Wilson County.

Jack and I were most fortunate to discover that the shift battalion commander was also the Chief of a volunteer fire department in Wilson County. Mike Brown is the Chief of the East Nash Volunteer Fire Department. The department which operates a fleet of two engines and two tankers protects a population of 2,200 in their 32 square-mile, rural community. They only have one major business, with the majority of their area engaged in farming or farming-related activities.

The department received their FIRE Act grant in 2003. They acquired a laptop computer, an LCD projector, an extensive array of training programs, five sets of turnout gear, an extractor washer for their gear, and replaced their old (older than old) radio base station. They also received 4 pagers and two hand-held radios.

Chief Brown then went on to explain that they also received physical fitness equipment and funding for medical examinations for every member. More importantly they have continued the medical examinations, using their own funds. "Once the people began to see the benefits of the program they got on board and became strong supporters. I have people who might not have seen a doctor since they were born. Now we insure that they are examined every year."

"Years ago, we had the unfortunate experience of losing a firefighter to a heart attack during a fire," Chief Brown noted. "Another member had a heart attack during a fire but survived. Thanks to the physicals we now have people we know are physically able to fight fires."

My friends, there are a number of things which we can never count. Things like lives saved, fires prevented, and injuries prevented are incalculable. How many lives have been saved by the FIRE Act? I do not think we will ever know, but if East Nash is any indicator, we are headed in the right direction.

This evening, Jack and I were the dinner guests of the crew at Station One, the headquarters station. I do not know how these folks keep doing it. Once again we were treated to a stirring example of firehouse cuisine. However, Don had a bit of a surprise in store for me.

As we were kicking back to enjoy another session of firehouse banter and BS, Don presented me with a nicely-decorated cake upon which the words, **Happy Birthday Harry** had been iced. He told me that although my 59th birthday was not until Saturday, he did not want the event to go un-noted.

After a slightly-off-key rendition of "Happy Birthday" I made the initial cut on the cake. Then one of the firehouse chefs took over and created 15 equal pieces. Then, as if by magic, a container of vanilla ice cream mysteriously landed next to my cake on the kitchen table. Way to go. Two of my favorite taste treats. Thank you gang, you made an aging fire guy feel really great.

My friends, the breakthrough work performed by the Wilson, North Carolina Fire/Rescue Service, thanks to the FIRE Act funding, will pay great dividends for our whole fire service.

They are out front on a number of operational issues. They are the future of our fire service.

Tomorrow it's off to Bedford County Virginia.

Bedford County, Virginia July 26, 2006

A Trip Over the General Motors Test Track

Today's journey took us northward out of North Carolina into the rolling hills of southern Virginia. Our journey up U.S. Highway 29 was well worth the trip. I love the way that the roads here are laid out. The miles seemed to fly by as we went up and down the many hills leading up past Danville.

I placed a call to our host Deputy Chief Lee Day, just as we were turning off of U.S. 29 onto Virginia Highway 43. I recall him saying something like, "Well, I guess you are in for some real country driving now." I believe that I sort of dismissed his comment. After 4,500 miles of all sorts of driving, I thought I was pretty good. Boy was I ever wrong.

If you are ever driving on a highway in Virginia, and you see a sign that says, "Road Narrows Ahead," believe the sign. Virginia Highway 43 was a series of winding hairpin turns over hill and over dale. All I needed was a dusty trail to recreate the

U.S. Army's Caisson Song.

It was a 1.5 lane road tricked out with striping for two lanes. I was doing pretty well until a major-league sized semi came whipping around a particularly sharp turn. After what seemed like a lifetime's worth of driving, we turned off into the parking lot of the Bedford County Fire and Rescue.

Bedford County is a rural area in Southwestern Virginia. It is located just to the south of Lynchburg. Approximately 74,000 people live within the 800 square-mile county. Chief Jeff Jones mentioned that the population in the county has been growing at an annual rate of three percent for the past several years.

Bedford Fire and Rescue is an umbrella organization which supports 12 volunteer fire departments and 12 volunteer rescue squads. Their 800-plus members operate a fleet of 150 vehicles out of 30 strategically-placed stations. The county organization provides command, logistical, training, fire investigation, and a quartermaster system. Chief Jeff Jones told us they try to operate a system which is, "responsible and frugal."

One of their fire departments is fairly unique. The Smith Mountain Marine Volunteer Fire/Rescue operates a fleet of seven fire boats. They have no land-based responsibilities. However, they are charged with protecting approximately 500 miles of lakefront property. Part of their grant in 2005 funded the purchase of 35 life jackets in addition to turnout gear, SCBA, thermal imagining cameras, and a mobile air compressor with lights. In addition to their marine firefighting duties, they operate a dive rescue team.

During 2005, the individual fire departments in the county received a wide range of apparatus and equipment. They received the following items:

- Type III Wildland Pumper
- Supply pumper
- Two tenders
- Turnout gear, high-ex foam generator, safety equipment
- Partial funding for a heavy rescue vehicle
- Three pumpers
- Mobile air compressor, lights, thermal imaging cameras
- Large diameter hose
- Miscellaneous rescue equipment and extrication tools

In addition, four of the individual departments came together to receive a regional self-contained breathing apparatus grant.

We met with the Assistant County Administrator Frank Rogers. He expressed his thanks to Jack and me for visiting their county. "We have a quality system," he noted. "A great deal of our success can be attributed to the support we received from the FIRE Act program."

He went on to state that, "we support our fire and rescue volunteers." During our discussions Jack and I noted that the Chief, his Deputy, and the assistant county administrator all reinforced the fact the each of the 10 percent matching amounts were provided by the county.

After the last round of FIRE Act grants, the county is now about 95-percent standardized around a common SCBA model. Only one department is still operating a different unit. The county is hopeful that there will be success in this years round of FIRE Act grants to address that shortfall.

In speaking with Chief Ricky Tuck of the Moneta Volunteer Fire Department Jack and I learned that the FIRE Act grant had allowed their unit to add a vital new service to their list of operational resources. "The new rescue and extrication tools allow us to deliver better service to our citizens," Tuck mentioned. "We had a considerable wait for help before the new equipment arrived."

This department was also able to leverage the grant resources in an effort to reach out to the community for further financial assistance. They have been able to use the FIRE Act funding to acquire a new pumper. They replaced a 1981 unit that was mechanically unreliable. "We used the FIRE Act funding as the starting point for our apparatus standardization program, "Tuck noted.

"We want to reach a point where there are a limited number of different units," Tuck noted. "We have a limited amount of training time. At one point there were more than a dozen different models for our people to learn. We hope to move to this new program with assistance from the county and from the community."

The county benefited from Moneta's new fire safety house which was funded by the FIRE Act in 2005. $6000 of the grant funds were used to partially fund a used tow vehicle for the house. "This is a county-wide resource," Chief Tuck stated.

Once again the FIRE Act allowed a department to update a number of critical areas. Chief Jones closed our interview session by stating that "the FIRE Act has allowed us to move the Bedford County Fire/Rescue out of the dark ages. We would still be operating with a mixed bag of SCBA, turnout gear, and rolling stock, if it wasn't for this grant program."

I want to thank Chief Jeff Jones, Deputy Chief Lee Day and his wife Pat for their many kindnesses during our visit to Bedford County. Now it is on to Baltimore for a couple of days off. I will be posting from the Firehouse Expo in Baltimore on reactions to my Road Trip.

July 27, 2006

Greetings from Baltimore

Today was not a bad day at all. Jack and I left the **Hampton Inn** in Lynchburg, Virginia this morning en route to the **Firehouse Expo** in Baltimore. I really love the rolling hills of southwestern Virginia. However, the signs that we were headed back toward civilization became obvious as we hit the Charlottesville, Virginia area.

We played dueling semis for many, many miles. The housing advertisements also began going up as we headed north. South of Lynchburg we saw condos going for the mid-$100,000 range. But by the time we hit Fauquier County the prices had jumped to the mid-$300,000 range. I started getting homesick over those sorts of prices.

One thing that I want to share with you involves the number of help-wanted signs we have seen on our journey. As we motored north on U.S. Highway 29 this morning we kept seeing **Help Wanted – No Experience Necessary: Just a Willingness to Help Others** signs in every county. The volunteer fire service is in crisis mode and we need to take this problem seriously. These signs tell the story better than I can.

Civilization came racing toward us as we moved across Interstate 66. As we approached the Fairfax area, traffic came to a screeching halt. We made about 5 miles-per-hour for about a half hour. Not that good my friends. There is a major league construction project under way just west of Fairfax. Proceed at your own risk.

Once we hit Interstate 495, we moved with a speed rarely seen in modern history (at least on the Beltway). We blew by Washington, DC in fairly short order. I can remember one evening when the half-hour trip we had today took me well over two hours. God bless the Washington, DC Beltway.

As we made our way over the roads today, a number of thoughts were running through my brain. Was I having an impact? Does anybody really care about the FIRE Act? I know that I do, but is my trip going to do anything? Doubt can be one of the outcomes when a person over thinks something. I guess fatigue is taking a toll on me.

Jack and I really need to hear your thoughts on the trip. Sadly, I cannot answer your comments on the Blog. To those of you who have posted comments, thank you. To each of you who have something to say, please drop me an email at drharrycarter@ optonline.net. I may not be able to answer you until I get home next month. I am working on a way to post the Road Trip question guide on the Internet so that you can download it, fill it out, and send it to me as an email file attachment. Stay in touch.

Now for a bit more on the people-helping people program I am working on. A few days ago I told you about a fire department in De Kalb County, Tennessee that was working with some really old, home-made fire trucks. I reached out to a Masonic brother to see if something could be done. My friends, it may be that next week I will have a story to tell about brothers helping brothers across the miles. I do not want to tip our hand until the deal is struck. However, it looks pretty good.

As Jack and I walked over to the convention hall to pick up our registration paperwork, a number of folks exchanged pleasantries with us and indicated that they had been following the road trip. That had a positive impact upon my negative thoughts outlined above. I want you all to know that I will be injecting as much of my road trip comments as I can during my program Saturday morning.

More from Baltimore tomorrow.

July 28, 2006

Baltimore Day Two

Today was an interesting day. Jack and I watched a number of people attempting to give money away. We also saw people just walk by them without pausing to even listen. People failed to read their literature, people blew them off. We watched this go one for almost 45 minutes. I had to stop by and mention the purpose of our Road Trip to them.

They are doing a really good thing. But people just thought that they were out trying to sell some insurance. The Fireman's Fund Insurance Company has established the **Fireman's Fund Heritage**. Fireman's Fund Insurance Company awards millions of dollars in grants each year for the purchase of equipment, fire prevention tools, firefighter training, fire safety education and community emergency response programs.

Fireman's Fund ® employees can nominate local fire departments and non-profit fire prevention organizations for grants. Employees are also encouraged to provide volunteer support for non-emergency activities.

Across the country, independent insurance agents and brokers that offer Fireman's Fund ® products can direct grants to fire departments based upon the size and growth of their business with Fireman's Fund ®. This fine company has also provided a tremendous amount of support to such national level organizations as the **National Fallen Firefighter's Foundation**, the **International Association of Fire Chiefs**, and the **National Volunteer Fire Council**. Since my tour is about funding from the FIRE Act, I thought that you might like to go to www.firemansfund.com/heritage.

Today I spent a great deal of time hiding out and napping. However, I did run into a number of people who have read my blog religiously. In addition, I bumped into Chief Steve Fletcher of the Gilt Edge, Tennessee Fire Department. He is attending a number of educational events and working the exhibit floor. There were members of the Wilson, North Carolina out working the Expo exhibit hall. I also bumped into Brian Blauer from the Illinois Fire Service Institute.

Tonight I made good on a promise to Jack. We went out for an Italian supper. We have been looking to eat Italian for several days now. A number of people at the hotel recommended **Chiapparelli's** in Little Italy.

They told Jack and I that the salad was to die for and that there was nothing bad on the menu. Jack and I want to add our stirring recommendation. The salad was outstanding and the veal was fabulous. I am thinking that August will be the month that I head on over to Weight-Watchers.

Anyway, I have tried to spend some time trying to build up my strength for the last week of the Road Trip. Tomorrow it is off to West Virginia. Take care my friends and stay safe.

Bruceton Mills, West Virginia July 29, 2006

A Happy Birthday in the Mountains of West "by God" Virginia

Saturday was a great day. It started with the program that it was my privilege to deliver at the 2006 **Firehouse Expo** in Baltimore. My message was about the need to attack the problem of the decline and fall of the volunteer fire service before it is too late. My message must have had meaning, as there was a standing room only audience in the room. More than that, no one left the room. It made me feel that my words are on target.

As I was on my way out of the exhibition center, I bumped into another one of my literary heroes, Hal Bruno. Hal is a veteran of decades of service to the fire and journalistic worlds. We spoke at length about the status of the FIRE Act and about my Road Trip. He urged me to tell my tale to all who will listen.

He and I also came to another agreement at this time. Each of us must re-double our efforts to write about this invaluable federal program. We need to bring the straight facts to a public that has been confused by the spectacular case of the "Dumb-Ass" created by the confused and biased members of the regular media who just do not get the fact that our FIRE Act predates the terrorist attacks of 9/11.

These misinformed and prejudiced reports are doing incalculable harm to our efforts to have the FIRE Act reauthorized and fully funded. My friends, if we do not get off of our collective dead asses, this program could go away. Hal and I agree that it seems as though there is a commando unit somewhere that is actively working to lie, cheat, and steal away our FIRE Act.

Heck, there are even people in the Department of Homeland Security who do not get it. Hal wrote about the fact that a DHS spokesman stated that the Bush Administration is against funding physical fitness programs, since fitness is an individual responsibility. What a load of camel dung. Anyway, Hal and I agreed that he and I will devote a lot of writing time to insuring that the FIRE Act lives a long and happy life.

At about 1145 hr. Jack and I hit the road for Bruceton Mills, West Virginia. Thanks to the absolutely perfect directions provided by our host, Derrick Crane, our journey went quite well. However, let me urge you to avoid the I-70/U.S.15 interchange in Frederick, Maryland. Whoa what a load of traffic.

Let me tell you my friends. I now know exactly why the sports teams at West Virginia University go by the proud nickname of the Mountaineers. As we entered western Maryland, the hills began to get progressively higher, and the valleys lower. After awhile, they weren't hills anymore. My friends, they were mountains.

Bruceton Mills is located just off of Interstate 68 on West Virginia Highway 26. It is a lovely little town which seems to be built into the side of one of the many beautiful hills in the area. Its 7,700 residents live within the 165 square miles of their lovely rural community.

Our host for the day was Derrick Crane who is the training officer for the department. Upon our arrival he introduced Jack and me to Randy Spiker, their Assistant Chief, and Firefighter Steve Bennett. We toured the fire station and then moved to their meeting room for our interview.

Founded in 1947, the Bruceton Mills/Brandonville Volunteer Fire Department is charged with providing fire protection and rescue services for approximately 1/3 of Preston County. Operating out of a single station in downtown Bruceton Mills, they cover a great deal of land area. Their 20 active members also provide fire and rescue services for about 17 miles of Interstate 68.

Theirs is an area without a great deal of industry, outside of small owner-operated businesses and their local banks. The primary businesses in the area are involved in the timber and forest products industry. There is yet another growth industry in the community. The federal prison system has built the first two new units of what eventually will be a nine-unit major prison facility.

Chief Spiker mentioned that Bruceton Mills is becoming a bedroom community for Morgantown. People who cannot afford a home in Morgantown are moving out to communities such as Bruceton Mills, which is located within easy commuting distance of Morgantown.

Derrick Crane noted that about fifteen new developments have been built in the past ten years. In addition both Derrick and Randy mentioned that about 150 of their 400 runs last year were out on I-68. The increased housing and the increased highway response activity are linked to their thoughts that the future holds more of the same. Each of our interviewees mentioned the fact that their new equipment allowed them to be better prepared to work on the Interstate Highway network in their area.

Their 2002 FIRE Act grant allowed them to acquire self-contained breathing apparatus and fourteen complete sets personal protective equipment. The new gear replaced some rather old protective clothing. In order to stretch the impact of their grant, they purchased the latest version of their existing SCBA equipment. This will allow them to use existing cylinders with the new units.

"We did not want to set ourselves up for a problem fifteen years down the road," Spiker said. "The cylinders we have are of the type which can stay in service as long as they pass their hydro-static test every five years. We felt it made sense not to leave the department with a problem which would pop up in the future."

Firefighter John Mayle told us that the new equipment was a real blessing. He stated that, "more equipment allows us to broaden our focus. It gives us more to work with. The old gear was real heavy however this new gear is really light and easy to work with."

Their 2003 grant allowed them to acquire large-diameter hose, adaptors for their pumpers and tankers, a 4"-relief valve for each unit, as well as a hydrant bag for each piece of apparatus. In 2004 their grant money allowed them to purchase rapid intervention equipment, a RIT bag, large-area search rope, rope equipment, a hydraulic ram, and a thermal imaging camera.

In 2005 their grant allowed them to install a vehicle exhaust emission system in their station. "Our people are a lot safer now that they are not being forced to inhale the vehicle exhaust emissions," Crane noted. "We do not know what damage these emissions were doing, but it is a lot better now."

Just as my interview with the Bruceton Mills/Brandonville gang was winding down, members of a neighboring department arrived to share their story with Jack and me. We got to meet with Chief Corky Thomas and Assistant Chief Perry Barlow of the Kingwood Volunteer Fire Department.

They told us that Kingwood was community of 5,200 people

living within their 52 square mile land area. Their department has 23 members and operates a fleet of two pumpers, a pumper-tanker, a mini-pumper, a rescue vehicle and a personnel carrier.

Their 2004 FIRE Act grant allowed them to acquire 17 new sets of turnout gear, as well as 17 sets of SCBA. Perry Barlow told me that they were operating with a variety of SCBA units whose vintages dated back to the 1970's.

"We were operating three different types of SCBA," he mentioned. "Since each was old and each operated differently there could be mistakes during a critical time. We are not as apt now to make mistakes since all of the units in service are the same."

Like Bruceton Mills, they acquired the latest version of their existing models. They did this for the same reason. They told me that they did not want to stick the future with a bill for something they did in 2005. They also acquired a thermal imaging camera.

Chief Thomas noted that, "morale in the department is up. It was like Christmas when all of the new gear arrived." Jack and I have heard this story or something similar in each of the communities we have visited. They also mentioned that their firefighting operations were more efficient now. Using the thermal imagining camera has improved their ability to complete extinguishing operations quickly and efficiently.

Each of these two fire departments conducts a variety of fund-raising events during the year. They also receive approximately $40,000 in state funding. It was their fund-raising efforts which allowed them to make up the matching portion for their grants.

Just as Jack and I were packing up our pads, pens, and cameras, Derrick Crane came into the room with a large white box. The folks gathered around as I opened the box. Therein was a beautiful birthday cake with red letters and a red fire truck which was a representation of their 1974 pumper. Believe me when I say that we left Bruceton Mills with fond memories of a fine group of firefighting folks.

Star City, West Virginia July 30, 2006

The View from the Mountain

Today was one of those luxury days similar to those we experienced in Baltimore. We are actually spending two days in the same **Hampton Inn** in Morgantown, West Virginia. It is so nice not to have to shave, shower, and scoot out of the front door toward the "Grey Ghost" after yesterday's trip to Bruceton Mills.

Apparently the Morgantown area was hosting some form of large-scale motorcycle rally. News reports indicated that there were more than 25,000 bikers in the area. A great many of them were staying with us at the inn. The folks we met here did not appear to be of the hard core biker variety you see in the movies.

The folks with whom I spoke were discussing their six-hour ride from Columbus, Ohio. The fellow I spoke with told me that his group makes a trip each month. He noted that this was a much longer ride than normal. These were some really special folks. They actually parked their bikes two to a parking space and made sure that everyone was wearing a helmet.

At this point I would like to pass along a word of praise to the **Walgreen Stores**. My friend Jack needs to take a variety of medications for a number of medical problems. Not to worry. All of his records were entered into the system at the Walgreen store in his hometown.

During our stops in Wisconsin, Tennessee, and West Virginia, Jack has had to avail himself of their services. At each location the service was prompt, polite, and professional. My hat is off to a company that can provide such a consistently great service in a wide variety of locations.

Our host Mark Mc Fall stopped by to pick us up at about 1130 hrs. He wanted to be sure that we had plenty of time to see the Morgantown/Star City area. Our tour of the city took us to a number of West Virginia University locations. Of course since Mark is a WVU alumnus, a bit of personal pride could be detected.

One thing that Jack and I saw which impressed us was the downtown monorail system that the university has provided to transport its students from the main campus to the Evansdale campus located on a hill overlooking the downtown campus. We also visited the medical center complex, the football stadium, and the basketball arena.

There is a great deal of development in the Morgantown/ Star City area. The sides of the hills are dotted with new homes and condominiums. The university has created a series of major research and medical facilities and the National Institute of Occupation Safety and Health of the Centers for Disease Control has a major facility near the university medical complex.

One thing that you should know is that Star City and Morgantown are rather neatly intertwined. Mark took us to his house in Morgantown. However, he noted that the house behind him is actually in Star City. A look at the map portrayed the true nature of this intertwined arrangement. Each department responds through its neighbors streets on the outer edges of their cities.

At about 1300 hrs, we met with Fire Chief Justin Quinn at the Star City fire station. I should point out that there is one heck of a drop off down the hill in front of the station. It runs down hill directly to the Monongalia River. It must be a real bitch when the snow and ice arrive.

Star City has a population of approximately 16,000 people within its 15-square mile response area. There are a number of major industries in the community, including a large-scale generic drug company, a major petroleum storage company and a wide array of mercantile and commercial occupancies.

The chief also noted that Star City is famed for its many glass factories, all of which are still in business. He mentioned that the city has an excellent water supply system and that more than 90 percent of the city is protected by hydrants.

The Star City Fire Department was founded in 1936. Its 40-member staff operates a fleet of two engines and a tower ladder out of a single station. Their 1967 tower ladder is up for sale and it will leave service as soon as the 1986 aerial scope they acquired passes its certification test. The two pumpers are a 1994 model and a 2005 model.

Annually they respond to more than 450 calls for assistance. In addition to their regular community fire protection duties, they provide protection for about 12 miles of Interstate Highway 79. The chief indicated that their new FIRE Act-funded equipment has allowed them to be better prepared to perform their duties on the I-79 corridor.

Their normal funding is a combination of state assistance and local fund-raising efforts. Chief Quinn explained that $40,000 of their annual $70,000 budget comes from the state's fire department assistance program.

They have received two FIRE Act grants. In 2003 their funding enabled them to acquire 15 full sets of protective equipment and 15 self-contained breathing apparatus units. They were also able to acquire 30 spare cylinders and sufficient extra face-pieces so that every member has their own. In addition they outfitted all of the face-pieces with voice amplification equipment.

In 2004 they received a FIRE Act grant that allowed them to install a full automatic fire sprinkler system in their station, as well as a complete fire alarm system. This was an important addition because the department maintains a bunk-in program. Students from West Virginia University live in the station and respond with the department when they are not attending class.

Once again Jack and I have seen a fine instance of where the FIRE Act funding has had a positive impact upon a local fire department. "Our people have been turning out a lot better now," Chief Quinn told us. "The new equipment has made our job easier."

Chief Quinn also noted that, "having the new basic equipment allows us to provide a better level of protection to our community. The new equipment is lighter and better. Our people now feel better and have more confidence in the new equipment."

Jack and I are now ready to head on out in the morning for the final official stop on our 2006 FIRE Act Road Trip, Wittensville, Kentucky. However, there will be a number of blog entries through the month of August as I visit other departments in New Jersey, Pennsylvania, and Delaware. I am also hoping to have a meeting with Congressman Pascrell when I get back home next weekend. More to follow my friends.

Morgantown, West Virginia July 31, 2006

An Addendum

Just before we took up out of Morgantown, West Virginia Jack and I stopped in to see our buddy Mark Mc Fall at the National Institute of Occupational Safety and Health (NIOSH) in Morgantown. He invited us to meet his buddies at the Firefighter Fatality section at NIOSH. What a fortunate happenstance.

It turns out that his supervisor at NIOSH, Robert Koedam, is the Fire Chief for a small volunteer fire department near Morgantown. The Triune Halleck Volunteer Fire Department protects approximately 4,000 people who live within their 40 square mile fire protection area, and support a rural district of approximately 100 square miles.

They have an annual budget of approximately $60,000. $40,000 of this funding comes from state sources. The balance comes from a variety of fund-raising efforts.

The department was founded in 1953. The 24 members of the department operate a fleet of one pumper, one tanker, a mini-pumper, and a heavy rescue vehicle out of a single station. They also protect a 12 mile stretch of Interstate 79 and Interstate 68.

They received FIRE Act grants in 2004 and 2005. The 2004 grant allowed them to acquire 20 full sets of protective clothing, as well as 12 new self-contained breathing apparatus (SCBA) units. They acquired 20 new face-pieces in addition to the 12 which came with the new units. Each person now has their own individual face-piece.

Their 2005 funding allowed them to acquire a wide array of wildfire firefighting equipment. They also acquired a thermal imaging camera and two portable pumps for their rural firefighting operations. Chief Koedam told us that, "we use these pumps in place of our pumper at the water source."

In addition, they received funding that allowed them to acquire over 300 smoke detectors and a compliment of fire prevention literature. "We were able to give away over 300 smoke detectors at a recent open house," Chief Koedam noted.

He also told Jack and I that there is no way that they could have gotten the new items without the FIRE Act. "We would probably have chipped away at our want list over the course of time," he mentioned. "However, there is no way we could have gotten it all at one time."

He told Jack and me that the department's morale is up and that participation in training sessions has improved greatly. "There is no downside to the FIRE Act," he said. "The FIRE Act grant program is truly needed by the fire service."

After a break for coffee and, Jack and I left for Kentucky.

Wittensville, Kentucky July 31, 2006

A Fitting Conclusion

Our trip down from the mountains was a really interesting journey. I am here to tell you that Interstate 79 south of Morgantown, West Virginia does not run straight for more than a few hundred yards. As I drove down the road, I felt like I was in a downward spiral, you know, sort of like an airplane coming in for a landing. It felt like Jack and I were on downward skein for the entire run from Morgantown to the state capitol in Charleston, more than 100 miles away

We finally hit some flat land just west of Charleston on Interstate 64. Once we crossed into Kentucky, the exit for U.S. Route 23 was upon us almost instantaneously. We were greeted at the border by the sight of a giant Marathon Oil Company refinery. As we made our way south we found ourselves being escorted by an almost continual flow of large tractor trailer dump trucks moving north and south on U.S. Highway 23.

The reason for this truck traffic soon became apparent. Just a few miles down the road we saw giant piles of coal, one after the other. They appeared to be set up for a 24/7 operation. There were also a number of large coal-fired power stations on both sides of the road. There were trucks and rail cars full of coal surrounding each of the facilities.

About 50 miles down the road, we passed the sign telling us we were in Wittensville, Kentucky. Our host, Assistant Chief Brian Jeffers had the doors to their station up and their newest pumper out on the apron awaiting our arrival.

As Jack and I walked up to Brian, I mentioned the heavy-duty truck traffic on U.S. 23. He welcomed Jack and me to "coal country" and told us that we had just traveled the nation's busiest coal highway. Brian noted that coal was still king in Eastern Kentucky. He got no argument from either of us.

He also introduced us to Gary McClure, the founding chief of the department. Chief McClure served as the chief for nearly 25 years. He is now the Emergency Management Director for Johnson County.

The department's quarters are a metal structure located right on U.S. Highway 23. The actual name of the fire department is the W.R. Castle Fire Rescue. There is an interesting story about their name. Back when they were founded in 1981, the members of the department were casting about for some land upon which to build their new station.

At that time, a local physician, Dr. W.R. Castle had just donated some land to the community to build the W.R. Castle Elementary School. After some serious horse-trading, they were able to get a piece of highway frontage land near the school, on the same plot. In honor of the good doctor, the department decided to name themselves the W.R. Castle Fire Rescue.

The 35 members of the department protect about 3650 people within the 42 square miles of their response district. Their busiest year for responses was 177. Last year they made nearly 140 calls for assistance. Normally about one third of their calls are for motor vehicle accidents. Watching the cars and trucks whiz by, I did not find his numbers hard to believe.

The department operates an apparatus fleet which includes two pumpers, a tanker, and a mini-pumper which doubles as a rescue vehicle. They are part of an active mutual aid program in Johnson County.

The department has applied for grants each time since the FIRE Act program was created. They received grants in 2003 and 2004. In 2003 they were able to acquire 30 full sets of turnout gear, eight new self-contained breathing apparatus units, and eight additional cylinders, as well as accountability tags for every member. In addition to these items, they received two RIT packs, a laptop computer, an LCD project, and a library of training programs and manuals.

Their 2004 grant allowed them to acquire a supply of new attack and supply hose, foam eductors, foam nozzles, and other new firefighting nozzles. "We were able to modernize our entire operation," Chief Jeffers mentioned. "We had SCBA that was nearly 20 years old, as well as a variety of different types of PASS devices."

"We were always worried that someone might not be sure of how to activate a PASS device if they had to," the chief said. "We now train to one standard, which makes it easier for everyone to learn the necessary skills to use their equipment.

Chief Jeffers also told us that the troops are now more comfortable in their new turnout gear. They also feel more confident in their ability to deliver an effective service to their citizens.

Jack and I were also most fortunate to meet Chief John Thompson and Assistant Chief Tim Collins of the nearby Rockhouse Volunteer Fire Rescue. This is a unique group among all that Jack and I have visited on our road trip: they are almost brand new. They were founded in 2000 and are still in the early stages of their departmental growth. Nonetheless, they respond to about 50 to 60 calls for assistance each year.

The Rockhouse Fire Rescue protects about 700-800 households within their 25 square mile response district. They were created to replace another department that went out of business. Their fleet consists of a 1974 pumper donated to them, a locally-made 2,500 gallon tanker, and a well-worn ambulance which they use as a rescue vehicle. "The tank for the tanker came from one place and the chassis from another," Chief Thompson told us. "A local mechanic put them together for us."

"People would donate helmets, coats, boots, and hose to us," Assistant Chief Collins told us. "We would have to swap out our gear when we sent people for their firefighter training. It was kind of embarrassing, but we did what we had to do to get trained."

Assistant Chief Collins took us to their first fire station. It was located in a barn that a local farmer loaned them on a dirt lane off of a small county road. They could barely fit into the doors, and had a steep drop off as the truck rolled out on runs. I had trouble turning the "Grey Ghost" around in front of the "station.

We then went to their new station which they themselves built upon a plot of land donated by a local business person. It is a work in progress. Jack and I were amazed at how much work had been done since breaking ground for the new station last September.

Their total budget is $23,000, part of which comes from the county and part from the state. They augment this with local fund raising events. "Our FIRE Act grant was a Godsend," Assistant Chief Collins told us. "We were wearing whatever people would donate to us. We would have spent years trying to buy new equipment."

The department received FIRE Act grants in 2003 and 2005. Their first grant allowed them to acquire 20 full sets of personal protective equipment. They also got eight new SCBA units and eight spare cylinders, as well as pagers for the members and two RIT packs.

In 2005 they acquired a great deal of training equipment and materials. They got a laptop computer, an LCD projector, and a monitor and DVD/VHS player. They also got a Rescue Randy and a CPR mannequin.

Assistant Chief Collins told us that the department would never have been able to buy the things they needed. "We never would have gotten ahead without the FIRE Act money," Chief Thompson added. "We now have pride in what we have."

W.R. Castle Fire Rescue and Rockhouse Fire Rescue are building close personal and operational ties. Many individuals belong to both departments. They work together, train together, and play together. All of their FIRE Act gear, SCBA, and equipment were purchased to the same specifications. They are committed to creating a local system of operational interoperability.

My friends, I can think of no better final stop for my road trip than that which I had in Kentucky. We started with a major incident in Hershey on July 6. We finished up with a small, rural fire department that is still in the infant stages of their fire service life.

Perhaps the sign on the front of the new Rockhouse Volunteer Fire Rescue station says it best for us all here in America.

Rockhouse Fire Rescue
The Desire to Serve
The Courage to Act
The Ability to Perform

The W.R. Castle Fire Rescue and the Rockhouse Fire Rescue are the exact sorts of agencies that this legislation was designed to help. We need to do all within our power to keep the FIRE Act alive and well.

After a supper of hot dogs and chili, Jack and I took off for our **Hampton Inn** in Ashland, Kentucky. Tomorrow it is off to Greencastle, Pennsylvania to meet with our buddies from the Cumberland Valley Volunteer Fireman's Association.

Chambersburg, Pennsylvania August 1, 2006

Reflections I

Today was a reprisal of yesterday's trip south. Let me assure you that it is very difficult to get lost on a road trip when you return up the same road on your way back north. Let me assure you that today's run was made without any particular pressure. We did not have the stress and anxiety of arriving somewhere and having to be on time for an appointment with our next host.

I have come to the conclusion that you cannot travel thousands of miles and meet with scores of people without arriving at a certain number of conclusions. I think that I will spend the next few days sharing some of my post-road trip thoughts with you.

There is so much to say that I think it is necessary to break it down into small, easily digested bites. This will allow me to compose my thoughts and then lay them out in a logical fashion. I will need to do this for the project which lies immediately ahead of me, so I might as well start now. At some point, I will have to create the journal that encompasses my findings.

Let me begin today's visit with you by sharing some simple

statistics. In the space of 26 days, Jack and I traveled more than 6,000 miles. We consumed untold quantities of food and drink. The "Grey Ghost" consumed one heck of a lot of go-juice. I also discovered that my EZ-Pass device works on the toll roads of Illinois.

We traveled through or stopped in 18 states, and met at 27 separate locations. Given the multiplier effect of the manner in which we conducted our interviews, Jack and I met with members of more than 45 departments.

Today I want to share some thoughts on the types of departments that Jack and I met along the way. You need to remember that I was invited to each place that I visited except one. I was looking for success stories and with one exception that is what I saw.

The first thing that jumps out at me from my findings is that not a single metropolitan-sized department invited me to see their success. I know of many who received FIRE Act grants, but I guess they did not see any merit in my trip. I will not speculate as to why this happened. I would hope that if I make another trip in the future that someone would ask me to stop by.

The break down of departments visited included 34 volunteer agencies and eight career departments. That breaks down to 17 percent career and 83 percent volunteer. None of these departments protected a major municipality. The largest city we visited was Johnstown, Pennsylvania. The smallest place was Longview, Illinois, population 200.

In each place I met real people. I met dedicated people who spend each day working hard to protect their fellow citizens and their communities. These are people who make sacrifices to insure that fire and EMS protection is delivered to the citizens they are sworn to protect.

No matter the location, Jack and I were treated as brother firefighters wherever we went. The door was always open and the coffee pot was always on for us. I just wish that the people in Washington, DC who make our laws and provide the funds for our nation knew more about the folks that Jack and I met during our road trip.

Perhaps that is one of the great things that will come from our efforts. The telling of a true story about the real people who make up our fire service.

Chambersburg Pennsylvania August 2, 2006

Reflections II

Today was a busy day. Jack and I attended the Emergency Response Safety Institute (ERSI) meeting in Greencastle, Pennsylvania, not far from Chambersburg. We did the important work of the institute in the critical area of highway safety. I would urge you all to visit our website at www.Respondersafety.com for the latest information on how your people should be trained so that they can operate safely on the highways of our nation.

I spent a few moments of quiet time today to reflect further on the things I learned during the course of the **2006 FIRE Act Road Trip**. Today I want to share with you another one of the trends that Jack and I noted as we moved across the country. It has long been my belief that there is no sense in learning something if sharing it is not a part of the equation.

We saw a number of instances where the FIRE Act brought people together. It actually built new relationships and strengthened existing bonds. The first instance of this came during our second stop in Johnstown, Pennsylvania. Our host,

Brian Feist had worked to create an informal group of fire officials in the Cambria County area.

Each of the people that I interviewed that day spoke of the interaction they had used to create their grant applications. In discussing this with Brian I discovered that these officers and members share frequent emails and meet once or twice a month to informally discuss matters of a common interest. This all happened because of their work on the FIRE Act grants.

I am fairly certain that this was something which was never envisioned by the creators of the FIRE Act legislation. I next saw this type of team-building effort at work in Xenia, Ohio. Perhaps the greatest success story of our trip came at this stop.

For years now, the City of Xenia Fire Department has operated on an 800 megahertz radio system. All of the other fire departments in Green County operated on a VHF system. One of the departments stepped forward to host a grant for all of the other departments in the county in order to come up to the 800 MHZ system already in place in the city.

Their successful grant effort resulted in an award for more than $900,000. This successful effort allowed the entire county to become completely interoperable. More than that, they have the necessary equipment to interact with local police, college and university, security, local and state highway agencies and a variety of other public and private entities. I believe that grants such as this broaden the impact of every dollar spent.

Our stop in New Knoxville, Ohio took us further down the same road of mutual cooperation. Representatives from the New Knoxville, Fort Loramie Community Fire Department and the Chickasaw Community Mutual Fire Company came together to tell us of their successful interaction.

They worked together long and hard to bring several rounds of grant money to their area. More than that, they made sure that when they acquired their equipment, all of it was completely interoperable. They also work together on various operational and training projects.

One of the amazing things that we learned during this session involved a recent major barn fire where more than a million gallons water was pumped. Our hosts shared with us the fact that of the 19 departments who had responded, 18 of them had received FIRE Act grant funding. My friends, this is what it is all about.

We saw this again in Alabama. There are a number of individuals in adjoining counties who came together in an effort to become better at writing their grants. There success was evident in the fact that each of the five people, from five different counties had received a new pumper. We also saw it in Virginia.

I would like to urge all of you to consider getting together with your neighbors. As you create your grant narrative you should work to demonstrate how funding for one community will have consequences that travel across the borders to broaden the impact of the proposal, or better yet how many departments will benefit from a joint operation.

Let me say the following to you in as strong a way as possible. Buddy up. Do not think of this as an "us and them" form of competition. Think teamwork. I would urge all of you to partner up in some way, shape, or form.

This trend toward coming together is a great thing. Jack and I saw it often enough to know it isn't a fluke. It is the product of the work of dedicated people. We need to stop fighting each other. If we fail to come together as a fire service, we risk losing what we have.

Chambersburg, PennsylvaniaAugust 3, 2006

Reflections III

By now you might be wondering what people have been getting with their piece of the FIRE Act pie? My friends, they have bought lots of wonderful new additions to their equipment larder. However, by and large their acquisitions fell into a number of major categories.

The top two items which we encountered most frequently came in the area of personal protective equipment (PPE) and self-contained breathing apparatus (SCBA). We did not log which brands were purchased by whom. However, rest assured my friends, all of the manufacturers out there are getting some of the action.

There were departments who would never have been able to afford anything new. We saw many people proudly posing with their new helmets, coats, boots, trousers, gloves and etc. We also heard some real horror stories about equipment that was donated to departments whose vintage ran back into the 1970's.

Thermal imaging cameras were another item we saw on many

occasions during our journey. These helped the departments to operate more efficiently. On many occasions these devices created mutual aid responses to those fire departments in the area who did not own this type of equipment. Once again, we saw FIRE Act money creating new partnerships.

Rescue and extrication tools were another item of choice for grant awardees. In a number of places fire departments were able to add response to highway rescue calls as a new service to their communities. That is another part of the FIRE Act which gets short shrift. The act allows departments to apply for funding to expand and improve the ways in which they serve the citizens they protect.

There are a couple of places which need to be singled out for special praise. In Johnstown, Pennsylvania, the fire department was able to use the grant money to construct a mobile communications command post. For about $60,000 they built a unit which is capable of performing in ways similar to units that can be bought for hundreds of thousands of dollars more. They can do satellite downlinks, and a great many other things which enhance and improve area-wide interoperability.

In Green County, Ohio, the FIRE Act grant they received created a seamless county communications system. They mated up new technology from the grant with existing 800 MHZ service and created a county-wide communication's network wherein everyone can communication with everyone else.

Talk about increasing their bang for the buck, they can talk with everyone else in the county, regardless of their frequency. They have created a true model of interoperability success.

Wilson, North Carolina is another community where a great deal has been done with communications. One of their grants funded a virtual-reality fire inspectors training program. This $750,000 grant has created a program that is now in use by more than 400 different fire departments in 47 states. This has allowed

FIRE Act money to make a difference throughout almost the entire country.

They also received another grant which allowed them to create an in-house teleconference system with equipment in every station. This allows for a more effective and efficient training operation. No longer do their people have to travel to a central location for their daily training.

Wilson has cut down the wear and tear on their vehicles. They have also lowered their fuel costs, and kept their suppression units in their neighborhoods. The citizens receive better protection when their neighborhood fire company is at home. Personnel now have more time for in-service inspections and other department-related duties.

Jack and I also heard a recurring theme as we moved around the country. People were so enthused about the new gear that membership morale and enthusiasm notched up considerably. During a great many of our stops we heard about how people had recommitted their efforts to their fire departments.

Adelphia, New Jersey August 4, 2006

Home is the Traveler, Home from the Road

The words of Robert Louis Stevenson best portray the feelings that I had as I pulled into my driveway here in Adelphia. "Home is the sailor, home from the sea, and the hunter home from the hill." In my case, the words might best be changed to read "home is the traveler; home from the road."

Do not get me wrong. I am glad beyond all belief that I decided to hit the road. The people I met confirmed that I am on the right track fighting for the FIRE Act. These were the average American firefighters who protect their communities and our nation day in and day out. I am so grateful for all who allowed me the privilege of sharing in their lives and the communities. I will be forever indebted to each of these fine folks for the many kindnesses that Jack and I were shown.

Let me also express my undying love and admiration for my best friend Jack Peltier. I cannot imagine how I ever would have been able to travel more than 6,100 miles all by my lonesome. The number of times that he kept my spirits up as I fought to get my words up for the day cannot be counted, but they were many. Many times it took the two of us to puzzle through the directions given by Yahoo Maps or Map-quest. I might still be driving around in circles were it not for Jack's help.

My wife and kids were glad to have the old Dadster home. My wife did a great job keeping the home fires burning while I was burning up the roads of our nation. The Adelphia Fire Company welcomed me home by allowing me to spend several hours on the road not long after I got home. We have made five runs since I got back. I missed more than 40 calls during my trip, so I have to work hard to get my percentage up a bit.

There are some folks to whom I owe an apology. Let me offer my apologies to my many friends in the Cumberland Valley Volunteer Fireman's Association (CVVFA). When I woke up this Thursday morning, there was only one word on my lips. That word was **"HOME"** and my desire to see my family was just too great.

Since Jack and I had spent Wednesday at the Emergency Response Safety Institute (ERSI) long-range planning session, I got to see a number of my friends. I also got to take part in some important discussions for the future of our highway safety efforts. However to those I missed, owing to my early departure, I hope you understand that after 28 days on the road, the urge to go home became overpowering. Rest assured that I remain committed to the good work of the CVVFA.

It took the better part of eight hours of diligent work to sort through the emails and mail that had accumulated during my absence. There are a number of phone messages that I will begin handling on Monday. There is also a lot of writing and consulting work that I will need to catch up on. I have to review and add information to about eight chapters of a book that I have been working on with Erwin Rausch. We are working on a new edition of our Management in the Fire Service text.

As I close this day's meeting with you, I want to assure you that there is more to do with regard to this Road Trip. Stay tuned to the Blog. While there may not be an entry every day, I know there will be some periodic updates. I have to meet with a couple more fire departments and I am hoping to set up an appointment with Congressman Bill Pascrell to discuss the FIRE Act. I shall be reporting on all of these things. Stay tuned.

Epilogue

The trip has been completed. The dream has been lived. However, life continues on. In the months after the trip, a number of important things have occurred. I believe it is important to share them with you, for many of these events have occurred as the direct result of the trip. Other aspects of things which occurred during this period have been the natural progression of life and the part which the FIRE Act plays in it.

I had the privilege of meeting with Congressman William Pascrell (D-NJ), the creator of the FIRE Act. I would like you to know that he was most appreciative of the efforts of Jack and me to publicize the good works which have occurred as a result of his legislation. He told me of his hopes for the future, and his efforts to increase the funding levels for the Assistance to Firefighter's Grant Program.

Jack and I were asked to help the joint FEMSA/FAMA Government Affairs Committee. Our labors along with Steve Lawrence and a number of other fine folks allowed for the creation of a website devoted to the FIRE Act (www.FireGrantData.net) and an excellent color brochure describing the successes of the FIRE Act.

I think it is critical for you, the reader, to know that the success of this program impacted more than just our fire service organizations. The fire manufacturing industry has seen a tremendous growth in their respective businesses. They attribute these gains to the impact of FIRE Act-related spending. After speaking with a number of industry leaders, I must agree. The FIRE Act has done great things well beyond the boundaries of the originally foreseen when the legislation was being crafted.

Good news has been the order of the day in many places.

Just before this book went to the publisher I was notified that a number of our trip host departments had received 2006 Firefighter Assistance Grants. In addition, Jack Peltier, my trip co-pilot called me to let me know that his department in Massachusetts had just been notified that they had received their grant. The same holds true for Donny Green of the Dekalb County, Tennessee Fire Department, Jerry Merges of the New Knoxville, Ohio Fire Department, Paul Doyle of Goose Lake, Iowa, and John Thompson of Rockhouse, Kentucky. The good works envisioned by Congressman Pascrell continue, and will do so until 2009 under the current reauthorization. Let us hope that we all can share in many more years of success.

Let me close this story about my 2006 FIRE Act Road Trip with a warning to all of you. Do not become complacent. Do not think that the program will always be there for us. There are those who do not like us and our FIRE Act program. They would steal our money and fritter it away on a whole host of things that will do nothing for you or me. If we do not maintain our vigilance and support, the FIRE Act can evaporate. Contact your Member of Congress and share this book with them.

Contact the Author

Dr. Harry R. Carter
P.O. Box 100
Adelphia, NJ 07710
www.HarryCarter.com
drharrycarter@optonline.net